MARRIAGE BONDS
and
MINISTERS' RETURNS
of
SURRY COUNTY, VIRGINIA
1768–1825

I0091041

COMPILED AND PUBLISHED
by
CATHERINE LINDSAY KNORR

Book Publishers

Southern Historical Press, Inc.
Greenville, South Carolina

Please direct all correspondence and orders to:

www.southernhistoricalpress.com
or
SOUTHERN HISTORICAL PRESS, Inc.
PO BOX 1267
375 West Broad Street
Greenville, SC   29601
southernhistoricalpress@gmail.com

ISBN #0-89308-256-2

Printed in the United States of America

To
My friends and customers
(synonymous terms) who
have kept me happily in
business for eleven years
with, I hope, mutual pleasure.

JAMES CITY - ORIGINAL SHIRE
1634

SURRY - 1652

ROBINSON'S VIRGINIA
COUNTIES CHART 6
PAGE 167

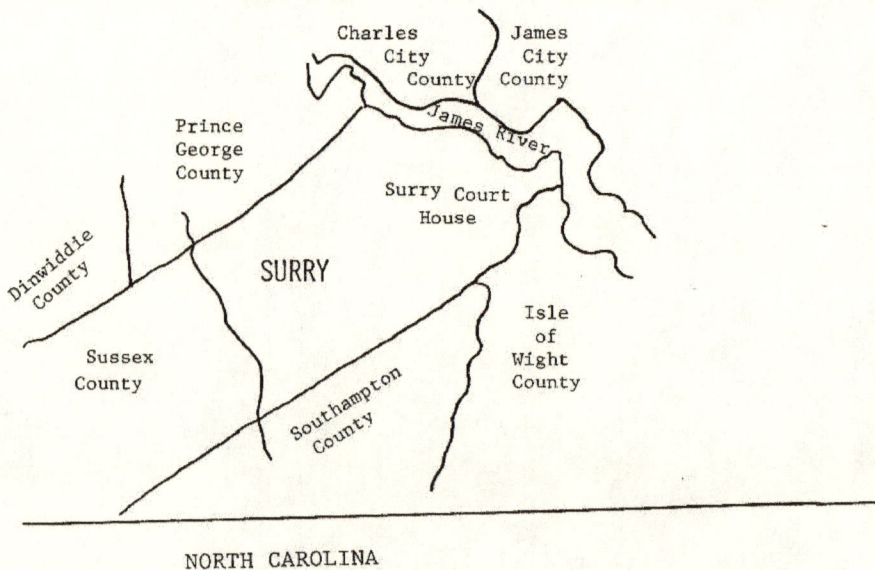

Charles City County · James City County

James River

Prince George County

Surry Court House

Dinwiddie County

SURRY

Isle of Wight County

Sussex County

Southampton County

NORTH CAROLINA

Publisher's Preface

Mrs. Knorr died in 1975, and after her death these books of marriage records were kept in print and sold by her late husband. Upon his death, they became the property of her grandson, Hal Wyche Greer, III, of Marietta, Georgia, who continued to sell them on a limited basis.

In mid-1981 I sought to find Mr. Greer to discuss with him the possibility of obtaining the exclusive publishing and sales rights to these 14 titles. In due time, Mr. Greer and I were able to negotiate a contract for my exclusive sales and publication rights to these books. It was agreed that Mr. Greer would have a final voice on the changing of the format of any of these titles when they needed to be reprinted. I suggested to Mr. Greer that when these various books sold out and a reprinting had to be done, that for the sake of cost, I would publish them in a 6" x 9" page size, but that the format and style would remain the same, and this was agreed upon.

The reader is cautioned to note that these new 6 x 9 pages are typed verbatum from Mrs. Knorr's original copy, and page by page, so that new indexing was not required. It was also decided that when a book went out of print, it would be retyped on an electric typewriter with a carbon ribbon for better legibility. As publisher, I felt it was important to call to the attention of the reader these changes and the reason for eventually bringing out all of these titles in a 6 x 9 book.

The Rev. S. Emmett Lucas, Jr.
Publisher

CATHERINE LINDSAY KNORR

PREFACE

Surry Marriages, judging by the many requests for it, ought to be my most popular book. One reason for that is that the Wills and other records have been published by Mrs. Lewis L. Chapman, Jr. of Smithfield, Virginia. To have available both Wills and Marriages rounds out a county so that the searcher has all, or almost all, the answers.

Surry County is in the very heart of that part of Virginia known as "The Cradle of the Republic". Lying just across the "Lordly James", Surry claims the distinction of having the English colonists land near what is the present town of Claremont on May 5th before they tied their ships to the trees at Jamestown on 13 May 1607.

There are so many historic spots one cannot begin to name them all. Smith's Fort Plantation, the Rolfe property, is part of the land that was given by Chief Powhatan to John Rolfe and Pocahontas as a wedding gift. Built in 1652 it is the oldest brick house in Virginia of authentic record. Here, too, is the house built by Arthur Allen about 1660 known now as Bacon's Castle because in 1676 it was seized and occupied by Nathaniel Bacon and his men.

Claremont Manor, Mount Pleasant, Four Mile Tree and Chippokes are other famous old plantation homes still standing and in perfect repair. So, too, is the old Glebe House of Southwark Parish. The ruins of the church are there and one grieves that the church itself has not survived.

For sometime this area was considered part of Jamestown as many colonists there had plantations "across the water". Soon they began to move across the river and live in what became Surry in 1652. One cannot blame them. Today it is a lovely, rolling, half cultivated, half wooded area and three hundred years ago it must have been a veritable paradise.

Formed 1652 from the original shire of James City, Surry first had representation in the House of Burgesses at the session of 25 November that year by William Thomas, William Edwards and George Stephens (Stanard's Colonial Virginia Register p. 69). Surry is one of the seventeen Virginia Counties named after English Shires, although spelled without the "e" as it is in England - Surrey. (Long's Virginia County Names p. 87.) The first sheriff was Thomas Swann. Surry's first Order Book is not extant so I cannot give you the names of the first Clerk of the Court, the Gentlemen Justices or the lesser officers.

When, as is always the case, discrepancies began to appear between the bonds as copied in the register and the ministers' returns as copied in the register, I listed about a dozen and sent them to Mrs. Lewis L. Chapman, Jr. of Isle of Wight County, asking her to drive the eighteen miles up to Surry and consult the original bonds to see which were right and which were wrong. She went to the Surry Court House, explained her errand and asked to see the original bonds. The County Clerk summarily and emphatically refused to let her see the bonds. A week later she tried again and was again curtly refused.

I had heard this was the state of affairs in Surry but had never quite believed it.

So, I felt I had no choice but to "go to press" with the discrepancies, cross referencing each. But, with my passion for accuracy I was not happy with such things as Shackleton in bond and Shackleford in returns; James S. Lane in bond and James Smith Land in returns; James Allen Bradby in bond and James Allen Bradley in returns; Nelson Bryan in bond and Nelson Bryant in returns. The answer to most of these riddles lies in the original bond.

Then I decided to try my luck and go myself to Surry Court House, a 1,200 mile drive. This held up the distribution of the book since it necessitated writing a second preface.

Surry Court House, a peaceful looking old red brick building, stands in a grove of venerable trees. Expecting a refusal I went in with no brief case, no notes. Introducing myself to the Clerk I asked to see the bonds. In an unexplained about-face she permitted me to see certain bonds but not to handle them. I secured my notes and tried to check them. It was not a pleasant experience. After half an hour of rather rough treatment during which time I offered to have the Surry bonds restored and received a curt refusal, I gave up and left.

During a delightful visit in Smithfield I lapped up enough courage, like the Cowardly Lion in the Wizard of Oz, to return to Surry and complete the checking. Enroute I had a bright idea. I asked Mr. Knorr to go into the Court House with me. His province was merely to loll against a desk and read the paper but be there. It worked like a charm and if things were not exactly as pleasant as a basket of chips at least there were no more insults.

Before leaving Surry I had occasion to go into the Bank and the proverbial Virginia courtesy and amiable halpfulness that met me there restored my confidence in Virginia graciousness so that, after all, I left Surry with a good taste in my mouth and a light heart.

I regret that I was unable to discover the denomination of all the Surry ministers. I identified two Episcopal Rectors, several Methodist ministers, one Baptist and one Presbyterian. It seemed to be a Methodist stronghold. My blak Rose who was kibitzing on the proof reading remarked: "Ef Rev. Nathaniel Berriman didn't do nothin' 'cept marry folks he'd a' made a good livin'." It's true, he was very active in the marrying business.

As always, spelling presents problems. No doubt Cocke, Cockes and Cocks were all the same. The French name Debereux is found Debrix, Debereaux and others; Kee, Kea, Key are for you to take your choice; Mallicote, Mallicoat and Mallicott; Riggin, Riggan; Sheffield, Shuffield; Rispess, Respes; all "by any other name would smell as sweet."

This book, as I told you in my announcement, is my swan song. They say a swan's last song is beautiful but sad. Mine is not beautiful and it is anything but sad. In fact it's downright happy. I'm happy because you have been such dear loyal purchasers of my wares and happy because I could bring my

beloved Virginia to your library, be it public or private. I
am happy to have increased the shelf space allotted to Virginia
by at least another foot. I am happy to have saved you transpor-
tation to Virginia to find out the maiden name of your great
grandfather's second wife. I am happy because in retiring from
this phase of my activities I am not leaving you comfortless.
There are four genealogists in Virginia carrying on the work of
publishing marriages.

Mrs. E. Burton Williams, 2702 Russell Road, Alexandria has
already published Louisa and Goochland and will soon publish
Amelia; Mrs William B. Wingo, 1230 Manchester Avenue, Norfolk
is doing Norfolk and promises Princess Anne; Mrs. James A.
Lindsay, 303 Gilmour Courtway, Richmond 21 has Henrico ready for
the press and Mrs. Joseph F. Major, 2231 Bancroft Place,
Washington 8, D.C. is working on Rockbridge. To Kathleen, to
Lib, to Joyce and to Nettie I will you, my friendly customers,
trusting that you will uphold them as staunchly as you have
supported my work, plans and dreams.

And so, dear people, I give you Surry. Because it is such
an old county and so important I wanted to give you a perfect
book but under the little Fort Knox atmosphere at the Surry
Court House the best I can do is cross references and a page of
decisions on what is correct. Sort of hind sight since fore
sight was refused.

Now I turn to clearing off a place to sit down in the
upstairs of this house. Don't laugh - every flat surface is
full, even every chaise lounge! To getting acquainted with
friends I haven't had time to see the last few years; to inspect-
ing the year old redecorating job at the Country Club; to writing
to my sons instead of keeping up the Bell Telephone Company.
In short, as Micawber says, getting back into circulation. I
might even try going to bed before 1 A.M. and I'm going to make
a conscious, cross-my-heart-hope-to-die effort to discover that
old fashioned commodity - leisure.

It's really all your fault; you kept buying and encourag-
ing me to work myself down to this happy and contented nub. I
love You!

(signed)   Catherine Lindsay Knorr

Confidential to Charlie: I lost my bet and will pay off.
I did not get along with Mrs. Virginia Savidge.

29 December 1813 James Atkinson, not Atkins.

23 February 1818, James Atkinson, not Atkins.

3 March 1821 Henry J. Bailey m. Elizabeth Williams, not Mary.

27 May 1806 Sherod Charity, not Shadrach.

31 June 1825 Stephen Collier m. Ann E. Cary, not Gray.

3 March 1813 Lemuel Emery, not Samuel.

24 May 1785 Henry Howard, Jr. m. Sarah Bilbro, dau. of John
     Bilbro, deceased.

18 September 1814 Miles Johnson m. Winefred Wright, not Elizabeth.

17 May 1819 Willis Presson m. Winefred Presson, not Boman.

9 October 1797 James S. Lane, not Land.

3 January 1825 John J. Pully should be William J. Pully

24 May 1808 Walter Spratley m. Elizabeth Shackleford, not
     Shackleton.

11 October 1808 Samuel Stewart m. Lucy Scott, not Lucy Charity.

     ALSO:

Rev. William Browne   )
)
Rev. Richard Dabbs   )   Baptist Ministers
)
Rev. Williamson H. Pittman   )

MARRIAGES OF SURRY COUNTY, VIRGINIA - 1768-1825

15 February 1810. Gray E. ADAMS and Mary W. Clark. John Bell, guardian of Mary consents for her. Sur. Joseph Warren. Wit. Rebecca B. Clark and Elizabeth Hamlin. Married by Rev. Nathaniel Berriman, Methodist. p. 82

11 December 1811. Henry ADAMS and Delitha Amiss. Sur. Edward W. Holt. p. 86

8 February 1785. James ADAMS and Elizabeth Barham. Sur. John Petway. p. 15

14 January 1800. Patrick H. ADAMS and Susanna Cocke. Sur. James Smith. Married 16 January by Rev. Samuel Butler, Rector Southwark Parish, Episcopal Church. p. 55

3 January 1803. Patrick H. ADAMS and Ann Hunt Bradby. Sur. William Randolph, Jr. p. 63

9 December 1811. Thomas ADAMS and Elizabeth Ellis "of lawful age", dau. of Thomas Ellis, Sr., who consents. Sur. Gray E. Adams. Wit. Polly Ellis. Married 12 December by Rev. Nathaniel Berriman, Methodist. p. 86

13 October 1795. William ADAMS and Hannah Judkins. Sur. John Judkins. Married 15 October by Rev. Nathaniel Berriman, Methodist Minister. p. 41

10 June 1814. William ADAMS and Mary Warren, dau. of James Warren. Sur. James Milby. Married 11 June by Rev. James Warren, Methodist Minister. p. 95

16 October 1779. Andrew ADAMSON and Sally Burn. Sur. Lewis Burn. p. 7

12 July 1784. John ADKINS and Elizabeth Campbell. Sur. William Cocke. Wit. Thomas Bland, Jr. John Adkins of Norfolk Borough. p. 13

21 December 1772. William ALMOND and Ann Wilson. Sur. John Wilson and David Donman. William Almond if Isle of Wight County. p. 1

14 December 1791. Samuel ALSTON and Elizabeth Faulcon. Sur. Nicholas Faulcon, Jr. Married 15 December by Rev. Samuel Butler, Rector of Southwark Parish, Episcopal Church. p. 33

28 June 1786. Thomas Whitmell ALSTON and Lucy Faulcon, dau. of Nicholas Faulcon who consents. Sur. John Faulcon. p. 19

23 December 1815. George ANDERSON and Mildred Edwards Williams. Sur. Nathaniel H. Williams. Wit. James Holt. Married by Rev. Nathaniel Berriman, Methodist. p. 99

20 November 1786. Nelson ANDERSON and Martha Smith, dau. of Lucy Smith who consents. Sur. James Smith. p. 19

26 April 1819. Archer ANDREWS and Eliza Peters. Sur. Jesse Peters. Married 9 May by Rev. James Warren, Methodist. p. 113

1

16 January 1797. Benjamin ANDREWS and Betsy Bailey. Sur. William Bailey. Wit. Ann Faulcon. Married 19 January by Rev. Nathaniel Berriman, Methodist Minister. p. 47

12 December 1811. Henry ANDREWS and Delitha Amiss. Married by Rev. James Warren, Methodist. Ministers' Returns p. 223

22 August 1815. Henry ANDREWS and Sarah Collier Bailey, dau. of Thomas Bailey, Sr. who consents. Sur. William Bailey. Married 24 August by Rev. James Warren, Methodist. p. 98

20 December 1804. John ANDREWS and Sally Scammell. Sur. Thomas Scammell. Married 24 December by Rev. Nathaniel Berriman, Methodist. p. 68

1 May 1799. Samuel ANDREWS and Mary Waggoner. Sur. William Bailey. Married by Rev. James Warren, Methodist Minister. p. 53

29 December 1789. Thomas ANDREWS and Amy Bishop, dau. of David Bishop who consents. Sur. Samuel Andrews. Married 31 December by Rev. Samuel Butler, Rector of Southwark Parish, Episcopal Church. p. 28

26 April 1791. Thomas ANDREWS and Rebecca Charity. Sur. Joseph Byrd. Married 11 May by Rev. Samuel Butler, Rector of Southwark Parish, Episcopal Church. p. 32

20 February 1815. Thomas ANDREWS and Faithy Walden, dau. of Drewry Walden. Sur. Nicholas Scott. Married 22 February by Rev. James Warren, Methodist. p. 97

9 March 1790. William ANTHONY and Lucy Bishop, dau. of John Bishop who consents. Sur. James Bailey. Married 11 March by Rev. Samuel Butler, Rector of Southwark Parish, Episcopal Church. p. 28

29 December 1813. James ATKINS and Elizabeth Young. Sur. Thomas Hardy. See James Atkinson. p. 93

28 February 1818. James ATKINS and Polly Hargrave. Married by Rev. Jesse Holleman. See James Atkinson. Ministers' Returns p. 229

22 February 1819. Barham ATKINSON and Sally Davis. Sur. Henry Rogers. Wit. Albridgton Atkinson. p. 112

8 December 1818. Ely ATKINSON and Ann C. Fitchell. Sur. John Clinch. Married by Rev. Nathaniel Berriman, Methodist Minister. p. 111

22 September 1821. Exum ATKINSON and Nancy Denson. Sur. Albridgton Atkinson. Wit. Lemuel White. p. 120

24 May 1804. James ATKINSON and Elizabeth Crawley Hardy. John Goodrich, guardian of Elizabeth, consents for her. Sur. John Dobbs. Wit. Philip Holt and John Stott. James Atkinson of Isle of Wight County. Married by Rev. Nathaniel Berriman, Methodist. p. 67

30 December 1813. James ATKINSON and Elizabeth Young. Married by Rev. Nathaniel Berriman, Methodist. See James Atkins. Ministers' Returns p. 226

2

23 February 1818. James ATKINSON and Polly Hargrave, dau. of
Pleasant Hargrave. Sur. John Holt. Wit. William Hargrave.
See James Atkins. p. 108

1 January 1823. Samuel ATKINSON and Elizabeth Hargrave, dau.
of Pleasant Hargrave. Sur. Isham Inman. Married 3 January by
Rev. Burwell Barrett, Sr. p. 124

12 November 1785. John AVRISS and Patty Newell. Married by Rev.
Henry John Burgess, Rector of Southwark Parish, Episcopal Church.
Ministers' Returns. p. 207

2 January 1798. William AVRISS and Agnes Austin. Sur. David
Booth. p. 50

29 August 1808. William AVRISS and Susanna Stewart. Sur. Carter
Marks. Married 4 September by Rev. James Warren, Methodist
Minister. p. 77

20 December 1809. John B.S. BLACKHURST and Margaret S. Wilson.
Sur. Samuel Wilson. p. 81

23 February 1774. Thomas BADGETT and Elizabeth Boradman. Sur.
John Jenkins, Jr. Wit. William Nelson. p. 3

10 March 1818. Robert H.I. BAGE and Rebecca B. Marks. Sur.
John Bartle. p. 108

21 December 1793. Thomas BAGE Jr. and Elizabeth Hart. Sur.
James Clarke. Married 24 December by Rev. Samuel Butler, Rector
of Southwark Parish, Episcopal Church who says Eliza. p. 37

26 July 1818. Thomas W. BAGE and Lucy B. King, dau. of Lucy
King who consents. Sur. Thomas W. Drury. Wit. G.W. King.
Married 28 July by Rev. Nathaniel Berriman, Methodist. p. 109

18 December 1819. Richard BADGETT and Martha W. Barker. Sur.
Joseph Williams. Wit. Priscilla Maget. Married 21 December by
Rev. Beverly Booth, Baptist. p. 115

23 March 1785. Edward BAILEY and Ann Hancock Putney, dau. of
Benjamin Putney who consents. Sur. Henry Lane. p. 15

24 April 1799. Edward BAILEY and Rebecca Marks. Sur. Francis
Ruffin. Married 9 May by Rev. Samuel Butler, Rector of
Southwark Parish, Episcopal Church. p. 53

24 January 1789. Henry BAILEY and Peggy Anguish. Sur.
Christopher L-cas. p. 25

8 December 1795. Henry BAILEY and Ann Foster. Sur. Thomas King.
Wit. John Marks. Married 10 December by Rev. Samuel Butler,
Rector of Southwark Parish, Episcopal Church who says Forster.
p. 42

3 March 1821. Henry J. BAILEY and Elizabeth Williams, dau. of
Thomas Williams who consents. Sur. Nathaniel H. Williams.
Married 6 March by Rev. James Warren, Methodist. p. 119

28 December 1786. James BAILEY and Mary Putney. Sur. Thomas
Bailey. p. 20

13 June 1798. James Cryer BAILEY and Ursula Bailey. Sur.
Benjamin Pretlow. Married 21 June by Rev. Samuel Butler, Rector
of Southwark Parish, Episcopal Church. p. 51

25 April 1809. James BAILEY and Eliza L. Dewell. Sur. Henry
Dewell. p. 80

15 October 1823. Michael alias Michael BAILEY and Elizabeth
alias Elizabeth Bailey, dau. of Isaac Bailey who is surety. These
are colored people. p. 126

5 March 1821. Richard H. BAILEY and Lucy Dewell "of lawful age."
Jane Dewell consents for Lucy; no relationship stated. Sur.
William S. Lucas. Wit. Howell Collier. Married 8 March by Rev.
James Warren, Methodist. p. 119

26 May 1823. Robert BAILEY and Betsy Debrix. Sur. Isham Inman.
Robert a free negro and Betsy a mulatto. Married by Rev.
Benjamin Holt Rice, Presbyterian Minister. p. 125

30 March 1795. Samuel BAILEY and Rebecca Brown, dau. of James
Brown who consents. Sur. William E. Batts. Wit. Thomas Brown.
Married 2 April by Rev. Nathaniel Berriman, Methodist, who
says Browne. p. 40

31 January 1785. Thomas BAILEY and Nancy Bailey, dau. of
William Bailey, Sr. Sur. Henry Marks. Wit. Josiah Gray. p. 14

17 December 1806. Thomas BAILEY, Jr. and Elizabeth Lascelles
Key "of lawful age", dau. of James Key. Sur. William Bailey.
Wit. James Key. Married 18 December by Rev. Nathaniel Berriman,
Methodist. p. 73

24 November 1823. Thomas BAILEY Sr. and Ann Slade. Sur. John
W. Spratley. Wit. John Slade, Jr. and Joseph Bailey. Married 2
December by Rev. Isaiah Harris, Elder in the Methodist Church.
p. 127

25 December 1811. William BAILEY, Jr. and Polly B. King. Sur.
Benjamin Andrews. Married 26 December by Rev. James Hill. p. 87

23 March 1814. William E. BAILEY and Nancy Holleman. Sur.
Wiley J. Delk. p. 94

21 July 1806. Stephen BAIRNS and Harriot Nimmo. Sur. William
Maynard. Wit. Peter Thomas Spratley. p. 71

12 December 1788. Benjamin BANKS and Mary Valentine. Sur.
John Banks. Wit. Joseph Roberts. Benjamin Banks "in his 23rd
year". p. 24

22 January 1803. Benjamin BANKS and Lucy Bruce, dau. of
Elizabeth Bruce who consents. Sur. James Roberts. Married 19
February by Rev. Nathaniel Berriman, Methodist. p. 63

15 March 1788. Jeremiah BANKS and Hannah Copeland Price. Sur.
Edmund Bennett. p. 23

29 May 1789. John BANKS and Mildred Valentine. Sur. Sampson
Walden. p. 26

2 March 1790. John BANKS and Mary Shearman. Sur. Jeremiah
Banks. p. 31

27 June 1780. Benjamin BARHAM and Frances Philips. Sur. John
Petway. Wit. Francis Young. p. 8

6 October 1804. Benjamin Judkins BARHAM and Rebecca Lane, dau.
of Walter Lane, deceased. Henry Lane consents for Rebecca;
no relationship stated. Sur. Nathaniel Davis. Wit. Amos Judkins.
Married 8 October by Rev. Nathaniel Berriman, Methodist. p. 68

11 August 1790. Burwell BARHAM and Silviah Pyland. Sur.
Thomas Pyland. Married 12 August by Rev. Samuel Butler, Rector
of Southwark Parish, Episcopal Church. p. 29

5 March 1823. Thomas L. BARHAM and Nancy Adams. Sur. Joseph
Barham. Wit. Patrick H. Adams. p. 124

1 September 1811. Willis BARHAM and Martha Savedge "upwards
of 21 years of age" dau. of Josiah Savedge, deceased, and Ann
Savedge who consents. Sur. Robert Moring. Married by Rev.
Nathaniel Berriman, Methodist. p. 85

19 December 1794. Benjamin BARKER and Susan Davis. Sur. Daniel
Matthews. Married 25 December by Rev. Nathaniel Berriman,
Methodist Minister, who says Susanna. p. 39

8 February 1800. Charles BARKER and Anna Carseley. Sur. Austin
Carseley. p. 55

26 December 1825. Frederick William BARKER and Martha Ann
R. Newell. Sur. Isham Newell. Married by Rev. Beverly Booth,
Baptist. p. 134

21 December 1793. John BARKER and Rebecca Bishop. Sur. William
Grantham. Married 24 December by Rev. Samuel Butler, Rector
of Southwark Parish, Episcopal Church. p. 37

16 March 1780. George BARLOW and Mary Lancaster. Sur. John
Harrison. p. 8

17 April 1813. Jacob BARNES and Nancy Carrell, dau. of John
Carrell. Sur. William Cockes, Jr. Wit. William Cockes, Sr.
Married by Rev. John Gwaltney. p. 92

2 June 1789. John BARTLE Jr. and Elizabeth Hazelwood. Sur.
William Cryer. p. 26

7 November 1818. John BARTLE and Sally Wilson. Sur. John
Faulcon. Wit. William Bartle and Thomas Carrell. Married 12
November by Rev. James Warren, Methodist. p. 110

26 January 1782. Thomas BARTLE and Mary Bailey, 21 years of
age, dau. of Thomas Bailey, deceased, and Mary Bailey. Sur.
Thomas Bailey. p. 9

27 February 1798. James BASEBEECH and Sally Cheatham. Sur.
James Cheatham. p. 50

25 January 1819. Drury BATTE and Mary Chappell. Sur. David Chappell. Married 4 February by Rev. James Warren, Methodist. p. 112

28 September 1791. James BATTERN and Mildred Davis. Sur. Peyton Emery. Married 13 October by Rev. Samuel Butler, Rector of Southwark Parish, Episcopal Church. p. 33

4 February 1793. Lemuel BATTIN and Patty Brown, dau. of Edward and Mary Brown who consent. Sur. William Bennett. p. 36

23 January 1787. Frederick BATTS and Betsey Lane, dau. of John Lane who consents and is surety. p. 20

31 January 1798. William E. BATTS and Elizabeth Wall. Sur. James Wall. p. 50

15 January 1810. Lewis BAUGH and Ann Cryer, dau. of William Cryer who consents. Sur. John Hart. Wit. John Bartle Jr. and Rebekah B. Clarke. Married 16 January by Rev. James Hill. p. 82

24 May 1803. Ezra BEALL and Sarah Moring "22 years of age". Richard Shackleford gives affidavit as to Sarah's age. Sur. Robert C. Maynard. Married 26 May by Rev. Nathaniel Berriman, Methodist. p. 64

7 January 1796. Nathaniel BEDDINGFIELD and Mary Waller "of age". Sur. William Bennett. Witl. Lewis Williams. Married by Rev. Nathaniel Berriman, Methodist Minister. p. 43

13 February 1775. Benjamin BELL and Edith Boake. Sur. Frederick Warren. p. 4

27 September 1796. Benjamin BELL Sr. and Martha Warren. Sur. Robert McIntosh. Married 15 October by Rev. Nathaniel Berriman, Methodist. p. 45

11 March 1812. Benjamin C. BELL and Martha Cofer. Benjamin Bell, Sr., guardian of Benjamin C., consents for him. Sur. Joseph Davis. Married 12 March by Rev. Nathaniel Berriman, Methodist. p. 88

5 March 1825. Binns B. BELL and Martha Ann Price. Sur. Samuel Price. p. 132

24 November 1807. Fielden BELL and Mary Graves. Sur. James Davis Edwards. p. 75

25 December 1781. James BELL and Winney Shuffield. Sur. Swan Lunsford. p. 9

25 March 1786. James BELL and Bramble Partridge. Sur. William Maget. Married 10 April by Rev. Henry John Burgess, Rector of Southwark Parish, Episcopal Church. p. 18

22 December 1796. James P. BELL and Rebecca Warren, dau. of Martha Bell who consents for her. Sur. Freeman Ward. Wit. Jesse Bennett and Samuel Berriman. Married 24 December by Rev. Nathaniel Berriman, Methodist. p. 46

15 January 1798. James BELL and Mary Warren. Sur. James H. Warren. Married 20 January by Rev. Nathaniel Berryman, Methodist Minister. p. 50

13 February 1807. James P. BELL and Sarah Davis "21 years of age". Sur. Samuel Davis. Wit. Cherry Davis. p. 73

27 January 1795. John H. BELL and Sally Warren, dau. of William Warren, Sr. who consents and is surety. Married 29 January by Rev. Nathaniel Berriman, Methodist Minister. p. 40

7 July 1818. John C. BELL and Margaret Edwards. Sur. Willis Swaltney. Married 9 July by Rev. Jesse Holleman, Sr. p. 109

2 January 1815. Micajah BELL and Rebecca Warren. Sur. Joseph Lane. Married 5 January by Rev. Nathaniel Berriman, Methodist. p. 96

28 November 1803. Samuel BELL and Elizabeth B. Gilbert. Sur. John Lane. Married by Rev. John Gwaltney. p. 65

6 April 1786. Stephen BELL and Jemima Ingram, dau. of Patience Ingram. Sur. Joel Thompson. Wit. William Ingram. p. 18

22 April 1806. Thomas BELL and Nancy Taylor "full 21 years of age", dau. of James and Sarah Taylor. Sur. Richard Gwaltney. Wit. Anthony D. White. p. 71

28 October 1823. William W. BELL and Mildred Price, dau. of Samuel Price who consents. Sur. William H. Ripley. Married 27 November by Rev. Isaiah Harris, Elder in the Methodist Church. p. 126

22 March 1791. BEN, a free negro, formerly property of James Jenkins and Susan Blizzard. Sur. John Andrew. Married 29 March by Rev. John Paup, Elder in the Methodist Church. p. 31

22 December 1823. James BENNETT, Jr. and Elizabeth Edwards, dau. of James Edwards, deceased. Edwin Edwards, guardian of Elizabeth, consents for her. Sur. John Bennett. p. 127

26 November 1796. Jesse BENNETT and Lucy Holloway. Sur. William Bennett. Married 22 December by Rev. Nathaniel Berriman, Methodist. p. 45

10 February 1784. William BENNETT and Elizabeth Waller, dau. of Edmund Waller, deceased. Sur. Philip Thompson. p. 13

14 May 1801. William BENNETT, Jr. and Polly Edwards. Sur. Thomas D. Edwards. Married 15 May by Rev. Nathaniel Berriman, Methodist. p. 59

23 August 1796. Joseph BERRIMAN and Kezia Holt. Sur. William
Holt. Married 24 August by Rev. Nathaniel Berriman, Methodist
Minister, who says <u>Keziah</u>. p. 45

14 May 1798. Nathaniel BERRIMAN and Martha Wilkins Judkins.
Sur. John Judkins. p. 51

25 October 1825. Nathaniel BERRIMAN and Sally Lane. Sur. Wyatt
Lane. Married 26 October by Rev. Beverly Booth, Saptist
Minister. p. 129

18 February 1817. Samuel BERRYMAN and Rebecca Bell. Sur. David
Davies. Wit. Judkins Warren. Married 20 February by Rev.
Nathaniel Berriman, Methodist. p. 104

27 January 1825. William H. BERRYMAN and Sally H. Seward.
Sur. John W. Judkins. Married by Rev. Beverly Booth, Baptist.
Return dated 28 April 1825. p. 131

28 January 1822. John BEVAN and Susannah H. Holt. Sur. Robert
Pretlow. Wit. Elizabeth Cornwell. p. 121

1 January 1801. Robert BEVAN and Hannah Harriss. Sur. Chapman
Harris. Married 6 January by Rev. Nathaniel Berriman, Methodist
Minister. p. 59

22 January 1793. Benjamin BILBRO and Rebecca Sorsby. Sur.
Archibald Davis. p. 36

26 July 1821. Patrick H. BILBRO and Louisa N. Lain. Married
by Rev. Beverly Booth, Baptist Minister. Ministers' returns
p. 234

6 June 1795. Thomas BILBRO and Mary Davis, 21 years of age,
dau. of Henry Davis, deceased. Sur. William Church, Jr.
Married 18 June by Rev. Samuel Butler, Rector of Southwark
Parish, Episcopal Church. p. 41

11 October 1797. Thomas BILBRO and Mary Lucas. Sur. Coleman
Harrison. p. 49

15 November 1806. Thomas BILBRO and Mary Stewart, dau. of
William Stewart, deceased. David Booth, guardian of Mary,
consents for her and is surety. Wit. Mason Bishop. p. 72

2 April 1825. Allen P. BINNS and Eliza Ann Barham "of lawful
age". Thomas L. Barham guardian of Allen P. Binns. Sur.
Patrick H. Adams. Wit. James Barham. p. 132

24 December 1799. William BINNS and Mary Slater. Sur. Henry
Crafford. Married by Rev. Nathaniel Berriman, Methodist. p. 54

11 January 1823. Archibald BISHOP and Barbary Emery, dau. of
David Emery who consents and is surety. p. 123

16 July 1818. Augustine BISHOP and Mary M. Bride. Married by Rev. James Warren, Methodist. Ministers' Returns p. 230

26 January 1824. Benjamin BISHOP and Eliza Carsley, dau. of Susan C. Carsley who consents. Sur. Randolph Whitmore. p. 128

7 December 1816. Braxton H. BISHOP and Patsey Bishop, dau. of James Bishop who consents. Sur. Pleasant Sheffield. Wit. Wilie Davis. p. 103

5 June 1815. Collin BISHOP and Elizabeth W. Judkins. Micajah Holt, guardian of Elizabeth, consents for her. Sur. Philip Smith. Married 7 June by Rev. Nathaniel Berriman, Methodist, who says Jenkins. p. 97

27 October 1795. Davis BISHOP and Rebecca Bishop. Sur. Henry Bishop. p. 41

27 September 1819. David BISHOP and Elizabeth Brockwell. Married 3 November by Rev. Beverly Booth, Baptist. p. 115

15 February 1788. Edmund BISHOP and Polly Bishop. Sur. David Bishop. p. 22

11 May 1812. Hamlin BISHOP and Sarah Bishop, dau. of William Bishop who consents. Sur. John Bishop. p. 89

7 January 1797. Harman BISHOP and Elizabeth Marks. Sur. James Bishop. Wit. Joshua Bishop. p. 47

26 December 1787. Henry BISHOP and Mary Austin. Sur. William Clinch, Jr. Wit. Archibald Davis and Elizabeth Davis. p. 22

8 June 1786. Hubbard BISHOP and Lucy Bishop. Married by Rev. Henry John Burges, Rector of Southwark Parish, Episcopal Church. Ministers' Returns. p. 208

20 December 1785. Isham BISHOP and Patty Bishop, dau. of Benjamin Bishop who consents. Sur. William Bishop. Married 24 December by Rev. Henry John Burges, Rector of Southwark Parish, Episcopal Church. p. 17

11 October 1791. James BISHOP and Mary Ekman. Sur. Sterling Hill. James Bishop son of Joshua Bishop. Married 21 October by Rev. John Fore, Elder in the Methodist Church. p. 33

28 December 1818. John D. BISHOP and Ann Ellis. Sur. Pleasant Bishop. Wit. Charlotte Pool. p. 111

28 March 1825. John BISHOP and Margaret Bishop, dau. of Mason Bishop who consents. Sur. David Bishop. Married 7 April by Rev. Beverly Booth, Baptist. p. 132

21 December 1802. Mason BISHOP and Susanna Bishop, dau. of Joshua and Elizabeth Bishop who consent. Sur. David Bishop. Wit. James Bishop. p. 62

22 January 1811. Moses BISHOP and Lucy Bagby. Sur. David Bishop. Married 23 January by Rev. James Warren, Methodist, who says Bagley. p. 84

18 August 1806. Stephen BISHOP and Frances Marks. Sur. Abner Marks. p. 72

29 November 1787. Thomas BISHOP and Fanny Davis. Sur. Joshua Davis. p. 21

1 June 1786. William BISHOP and Frances Greswit. Married by Rev. Henry John Burges, Rector of Southwark Parish, Episcopal Church. Ministers' Returns. p. 208

27 February 1792. William BISHOP and Mary Meads. Sur. Archer Holt. p. 34

22 November 1788. Wyatt BISHOP and Elizabeth Cheatham "of age". Sur. Archer Moody. Wit. Sarah Cheatham and Rebecca Moody. p. 24

31 July 1797. John BLASINGAME and Dolly Sledge. Sur. Jesse Dewell. p. 48

22 December 1817. Benjamin BLIZARD and Keziah Slade. Sur. John Bruce. Married 25 December by Rev. Nathaniel Berriman, Sr., Methodist who says Blizzard. p. 107

30 September 1791. Peter BLIZZARD and Mary Charity. Sur. William C. Partain. p. 33

28 December 1807. Samuel BLIZZARD and Caty Williams, dau. of James Williams who consents. Sur. David Charity. Married 7 January 1808 by Rev. James Warren, Methodist Minister. p. 75

14 November 1823. Henry BLOW and Ann F. Judkins. Sur. William E. B. Ruffin. Married by Rev. John Blunt, Deacon in the Methodist Church. p. 126

28 January 1789. Samuel BLOW and Mary Ridley Hart. Sur. John Ellis. p. 25

25 November 1790. Benjamin BLUNT and Ann Edwards. Sur. William Edwards. Married by Rev. Samuel Butler, Rector of Southwark Parish, Episcopal Church. p. 30

19 August 1806. John BLUNT and Ann McIntosh, dau. of Robert McIntosh who consents and is surety. p. 72

29 August 1810. Michael BLUNT and Lucy Trusty. Sur. David Trusty. Married 5 September by Rev. Nathaniel Berriman, Methodist Minister. p. 83

4 May 1807. Richard BLUNT and Jane Cocke. Sur. Richard Cocke.
p. 74

24 June 1800. Alexander BOOTH and Tempy Hix, dau. of Joseph
Hix who consents. Sur. David Booth. Wit. Daniel Porter. p. 57

7 August 1818. Alexander BOOTH and Sarah Emery "of lawful age".
Sur. John Stiles. Wit. Matthew Booth. p. 109

21 January 1819. Beverly BOOTH and Mary Cornwell. Sur.
Jonathan Ellis. Wit. Daniel Presson. p. 112

26 January 1802. David BOOTH and Susanna Sorsby, dau. of
Stephen Sorsby, deceased. Archibald Davis, guardian of Susanna
consents for her. Sur. Beverly Booth. p. 60

24 January 1820. David BOOTH and Ann Holleman. Sur. Wyatt
Lane. Married 10 February by Rev. Beverly Booth, Baptist. p. 116

18 December 1788. George BOOTH and Mary Eldridge. Nathan
Jones, guardian of Mary, consents for her and is surety. p. 24

14 November 1809. Mark BOOTH and Rebecca D. Watkins "of
lawful age". Sur. Robert Booth. Wit. Thomas Carseley. p. 81

7 August 1815. Matthew BOOTH and Rebekah Johnson "of lawful
age". Sur. Foster Cook. Wit. David Cocke. p. 97

22 August 1825. Matthew BOOTH and Harriott Bishop, dau. of
James Bishop who consents. Sur. Beverly Booth. p. 133

1 January 1824. Richard BOOTH and Elizabeth Bevan. Sur.
John Harris. Married 29 January by Rev. Burwell Barrett. p. 128

29 September 1810. Robert BOOTH and Rebecca Sheffield "of
lawful age". Sur. Nicholas Hite. Wit. Stephen Lucas. p. 83

23 December 1816. Samuel BOOTH and Sally Ellis. Sur. David
Booth. p. 103

5 February 1813. John BOWDEN and Sally Edwards Browne. Sur.
John Faulcon. p. 91

22 January 1816. Dempsey BOWERS and Martha Holdsworth. Sur.
Michael Rogers. Wit. James Briggs. p. 100

23 September 1803. Fitzhugh BOWLES and Susanna Barker, widow
of Benjamin Barker nee Susan Davis. Sur. Archibald W. Bowles.
Wit. Henry Johnson. Married 29 September by Rev. Beverly
Booth, Baptist Minister who. says Mrs. Susanna Barker. p. 64

5 January 1820. Pleasant F. BOYD and Margaret M. Sinclair.
Sur. Edward Cocke. Married 6 January by Rev. Nathaniel Berriman,
Methodist. p. 116

13 March 1775. Joel BOYKIN and Sarah Grantham. Sur. Thomas
Grantham. p. 4

22 December 1813. Simon BOYKIN and Anna Clinch. Sur. James
Clinch. Married 24 December by Rev. Nathaniel Berriman,
Methodist. p. 93

18 February 1784. James Allen BRADBY and Ann Hunt Cocke, dau.
of Allen Cocke, deceased. Sur. Richard Cocke, Jr. p. 13

5 February 1793. Richard H. BRADFORD and Peggy Hay. Sur.
Nicholas Faulcon, Jr. p. 36

13 December 1786. John BRIGGS and Mary Holdsworth. Sur.
Benjamin Cocke. p. 20

23 March 1790. Britain BRITT and Pamelia Andrews, dau. of
William Andrews who consents and is surety. p. 28

24 November 1823. William B. BRITTAN and Louisa Collier, dau.
of Benjamin Collier who consents and is surety. p. 127

27 April 1799. Samuel BROADNAX and Elizabeth Cocke. Sur.
Wilie Jones. Married 28 April by Rev. Samuel Butler, Rector
of Southwark Parish, Episcopal Church. p. 53

28 May 1805. James BROCKWELL and Elizabeth Bailey. Sur. Thomas
Bailey Jr. Wit. William Bailey and Thomas Bailey, Sr. p. 69

21 July 1814. James BROCKWELL and Willa A. Duell. Married
by Rev. James Warren, Methodist. Ministers' Returns p. 225

26 August 1806. Jesse BROCKWELL and Susanna Emery. Sur. David
Emery. p. 72

11 February 1819. John BROCKWELL and Margaret Casley. Married
by Rev. James Warren, Methodist. Ministers' Returns p. 231

18 August 1807. Littleberry BROCKWELL and Lucy Emery, dau. of
David Emery who consents and is surety. p. 74

12 January 1813. Allen, alias Allen BROWN, a free negro and
not of full age and Debby, a free negro raised by Thomas Pretlow.
Dau. Lucy James. Sur. John Faulcon. p. 91

18 March 1785. Jesse BROWN and Pamelia Davis. Sur. Samuel
Rowell. p. 15

18 October 1790. John H. BROWN and Elizabeth Jimm, dau. of
Jennett Jimm who consents. Sur. Henry Brown. Wit. Will Salter,
John Southall, William Thompson and John Anthony. p. 29

25 March 1783. Richard Dixon BROWN and Jane Gray. Sur. Robert
Hunnicutt. Wit. John Judkins. p. 11

28 March 1809. Scipio BROWN and Amy Johnson, dau. of Moses
Johnson. Sur. Benjamin Sampson. Wit. Joshua Womwell. Scipio
and Amy free negroes. p. 81

24 May 1819. Abram BROWNE and Tacy Bailey. Sur. Peyton Butler.
Wit. Thomas Harriss. p. 114

23 December 1785. Benjamin BROWNE and Anne Cocke, dau. of
Hartwell Cocke, deceased. Consent of her brother John Hartwell
Cocke. Sur. William Browne. Married 24 December by Rev. Henry
John Burges, Rector of Southwark Parish, Episcopal Church. p. 17

27 February 1812. Benjamin BROWNE and Susanna Lane. Sur.
Solomon Lane. Married 3 March by Rev. Nathaniel Berriman,
Methodist. p. 88

25 January 1803. Thomas BROWNE and Sally D. Inman. Sur.
Micajah Holt. Married 3 February by Rev. Drewry Lane. p. 63

1 November 1784. William BROWNE and Dolly Hay. Sur. William
Browne, Jr. p. 13

20 September 1792. William BROWNE and Elizabeth Ruffin. Sur.
Benjamin E. Browne. Married 22 September by Rev. Samuel Butler,
Rector of Southward Parish, Episcopal Church. p. 35

22 April 1817. William H.T. BROWNE and Susanna Ruffin. Sur.
Charles H. Graves. p. 105

24 December 1812. John BRUCE and Elizabeth Cypress "both of
age". Sur. Benjamin Banks. Wit. Samuel Blizzard. Married
2 January 1813 by Rev. Nathaniel Berriman, Methodist. p. 90

8 September 1825. Matthew BRUCE and Harriott Bishop. Married
by Rev. Beverly Booth, Baptist. Ministers' Returns p. 238

10 September 1808. Nelson BRYAN and Sally Slade, dau. of
William Slade who consents. Sur. William Slade, Jr. See
Nelson Bryant. p. 77

5 December 1822. Hamlin BRYANT and Susanna E. Cocks, dau.
of Benjamin Cocks. Sur. Peter Cocks. Wit. Matthew Booth.
p. 123

25 March 1791. John BRYANT and Rebecca Slade, dau. of William
Slade, Sr. who consents. Sur. William Slade Jr. and John Slade,
Jr. Wit. Thomas Riggan. p. 31

15 September 1808. Nelson BRYANT and Sally Slade. Married by Rev. Nathaniel Berriman, Methodist. See Nelson Bryan. Ministers' Returns p. 222

6 January 1808. John BURGESS and Susanna Warren, dau. of James Warren. Sur. Miles Burgess. Married 7 January by Rev. James Warren, Methodist. p. 76

24 June 1822. John C. BURGESS and Mariam H. Bilbro. Sur. David Booth. p. 122

31 January 1825. Miles BURGESS and Sarah Cooper. Sur. George C. Collier. Married by Rev. Beverly Booth, Baptist. Return dated 7 April 1825. p. 131

19 April 1796. James BURROW and Lucy Shall. Sur. William Arviss. p. 44

13 July 1796. Edward BURT and Elizabeth Judkins. Sur. Jacob Judkins. Married 14 July by Rev. Samuel Butler, Rector of Southwark Parish, Episcopal Church. p. 44

25 September 1789. Lewis BURWELL and Elizabeth Harrison. Sur. Samuel Butler. Wit. Jacob Faulcon. Lewis Burwell of Mecklenburg County. Married by Rev. Samuel Butler, Rector of Southwark Parish, Episcopal Church. Return dated 13 November 1789. p. 27

14 May 1796. Eleazer BUTLER and Mildred Johnson. Sur. Charles Holdsworth. p. 44

24 May 1819. Peyton BUTLER and Morning Bailey. Sur. Abram Brown. Wit. Micajah Holt. p. 113

8 November 1805. Reuben BUTLER and Elizabeth Ruffin, dau. of Francis Ruffin, deceased. Sur. Thomas Edwards. p. 70

30 June 1797. Rev. Samuel BUTLER and Martha R. Cocke. Sur. Wilson E. Wallis. p. 48

15 March 1803. Charles BUTTS and Ann R. Holt. Sur. Rowland Holt. p. 63

29 September 1807. Edward BUTTS and Ann Lamb Judkins. Sur. James D. Edwards. Married 1 October by Rev. Nathaniel Berriman, Methodist. p. 75

23 December 1816. Joseph BYRD and Betsy Andrews, dau. of Thomas Jones. Sur. John Charity. Groom's name also spelled Burd. p. 103

23 March 1779. Archibald CAMPBELL and Betsy Harris. Sur. William Short. Wit. Francis Young. p. 6

12 September 1801. Colin CAMPBELL and Margaret D. Wilson. Sur. William Cocke. p. 59

23 December 1797. Joseph CANADA and Tabitha Scott, dau. of Nicholas Scott who consents. Sur. William Scott. Wit. James Bailey. p. 49

CANIDA: See Canniday

20 February 1799. Jones CANNIDAY and Fanny Scott. Sur. William Scott. Married by Rev. James Warren, Methodist Minister who says "Canida". p. 52

26 May 1817. Gray CARRELL and Polly Pierce. Sur. John Carrell. Married 12 June by Rev. Nathaniel Berriman, Sr., Methodist. p. 105

_____ 1814. James CARRELL and Delphy Gwaltney. Married by Rev. John Gwaltney. See James Carroll. Ministers' Returns p. 225

16 May 1789. John CARRELL and Rebecca Smith. Sur. John Warren, Jr. Wit. John Moring and John Cocke. p. 26

23 September 1818. Jesse J. CARRELL and Polly M. Seward. Sur. John N. Carrell. Wit. John Seward. Married 24 September by Rev. Nathaniel Berriman, Methodist. p. 109

26 February 1811. John CARRELL, Jr. and Lucy Edwards. Sur. James Edwards. Wit. William Cocke, Jr. and William Cocke, Sr. Married 28 February by Rev. Nathaniel Berriman, Methodist. p. 84

21 December 1819. John CARRELL and Susanna Andrews. Sur. Wiley T. Savedge. Wit. Thomas King. Married 26 December by Rev. James Warren, Methodist. p. 115

20 January 1782. Joseph CARRELL and Molly Davis. Sur. Thomas Davis. Wit. David Cocke. p. 9

11 May 1799. Joseph CARRELL and Peggy Davis "of age". Sur. Richard Pierce. Wit. Susa Sorsby. p. 53

9 April 1810. Peter CARRELL and Anner H. Newsom "of lawful age". Sur. Matthew Booth. Wit. John H. Howard. p. 83

4 February 1785. Samuel CARRELL and Susanna Bridges. Sur. William Thompson. Wit. Thomas Spratley. p. 15

29 November 1787. Samuel CARRELL and Patty Collier. Sur. John Bartle, Jr. p. 22

25 December 1820. Thomas R. CARRELL and Nancy Stacy "21 years of age". Sur. Jesse J. Carrell. Wit. Hardy Harris. p. 118

28 July 1819. William CARRELL and Rebecca Carrell, dau. of
John Carrell who consents. Sur. Jesse J. Carrell. Married 29
July by Rev. Nathaniel Berriman, Methodist. p. 114

23 June 1823. William S. CARRELL and Sally W. Warren, dau. of
D.P. Warren who consents. Sur. Richard Murfee. p. 125

23 March 1813. James CARROLL and Delphia Ward "of lawful age".
Sur. Joel Thomas. James Carroll of Isle of Wight County.
See James Carrell. p. 91

22 November 1808. Augustine CARSELEY and Jane Kee. Sur. Thomas
Carseley. Married 9 December by Rev. Nathaniel Berriman,
Methodist. p. 78

11 June 1794. Hartwell CARSELEY and Rebecca Burgess. Sur.
John Burgess. Married 12 June by Rev. Samuel Butler, Rector
of Southwark Parish, Episcopal Church. p. 38

21 December 1814. Thomas CARSELEY and Margaret Scammell.
Sur. John Scammell. Married 22 December by Rev. Nathaniel
Berriman, Methodist. p. 96

4 December 1811. William CARSELEY and Polly Ellis. Sur.
John Velvin. Married 19 December by Rev. James Hill who says
Mary Ellis. p. 86

3 May 1782. John CARSLEY and Lucy Averis, dau. of John Averis,
who consents. Sur. Jacob Faulcon. p. 10

10 June 1819. John CARSLEY and Rebecca Pettett. Sur. William
Shelby. Wit. John James. John Carsley of Isle of Wight County.
p. 114

28 November 1820. Nicholas CARSLEY and Sarah Justiss. Sur.
Benjamin Cocks. Married 29 November by Rev. Beverly Booth,
Baptist, who says Carseley and Justice. p. 117

22 November 1812. Champion CARTER and Polly Hodges. Edwin
Edwards, guardian of Polly consents for her. Sur. Willis
Thompson. Wit. Josiah Holleman. Married by Rev. Nathaniel
Berriman, Methodist. p. 90

14 October 1803. Hamlin CARTER and Nancy Williams, dau. of
John Williams. Sur. Richard Carter. Wit. Penelope Smalley.
Married 15 October by Rev. Nathaniel Berriman, Methodist. p. 65

13 September 1809. Hamlin CARTER and Elizabeth W. Holt.
Sur. Willis Thompson. Married 15 September by Rev. Nathaniel
Berriman, Methodist. p. 81

20 January 1817. Hamlin CARTER and Eliza Ingram. Sur. William Ingram. Married 21 January by Rev. Nathaniel Berriman, Methodist. p. 103

8 January 1812. Jesse CARTER and Lucy C. Bell. Sur. Micajah Bell. Married 9 January by Rev. Nathaniel Berriman, Methodist. p. 87

14 November 1787. Richard CARTER and Sarah Little. Sur. John Little. p. 21

18 June 1817. William CARTER and Elizabeth Adams "of lawful age". Sur. Thomas L. Barham. Wit. Joseph Barham. Married 19 June by Rev. Nathaniel Berriman, Sr., Methodist. p. 105

29 November 1820. William CARTER and Lucinda Seaver. Sur. Benjamin W. Elensworth. p. 130

19 April 1799. Joseph CARY and Sarah Smedle. Sur. Richard Pyland. Wit. Will Adams. p. 53

29 December 1804. London CARY and Judy Harrison. Sur. Nicholas Faulcon. Bond written "London, alias London Cary and Judy, alias Judy Harrison." These may be colored people. p. 68

29 March 1819. Andrew CELSEY and Elizabeth Hix. Married by Rev. James Warren, Methodist. See Andrew Kelsey. Ministers' Returns p. 231

22 June 1807. Samuel CHAPMAN and Priscilla Madders "of lawful age". Sur. Thomas Maddera. Wit. Nancy Chapman. Married 23 June by Rev. Nathaniel Berriman, Methodist. p. 74

27 December 1809. Howell CHAPPELL and Sally Judkins, dau. of James Judkins, who consents. Sur. Joseph Judkins. p. 81

12 June 1800. Alexander CHARITY and Polly Debrix. Married by Rev. James Warren, Methodist Minister. See Ellick Charity. Ministers' Returns p. 216

5 September 1803. Benjamin CHARITY and Sarah Stephens. Sur. William Scott. p. 64

26 January 1818. David CHARITY and Polly Howell. Sur. John Charity. p. 107

29 January 1803. Elijah CHARITY and Charlotte Charity "of lawful age". Sur. Joseph Roberts. Wit. Henry Dewell. p. 63

12 June 1800. Ellick CHARITY and Polly Debrix, dau. of John Debrix. Sur. Aaron Taylor. Wit. Edward (illegible). See Alexander Charity. p. 56

24 December 1813. Henry CHARITY and Matilda Banks "above 21 years of age". Sur. William Ingram. Wit. John Williams. Married 25 December by Rev. Nathaniel Berriman, Methodist. p. 93

2 September 1807. John CHARITY, Jr. and Lucretia Charity, dau. of Rebecca Andrews who consents. Sur. David Charity. Wit. Miles Burgess and Nancy Burgess. (Thomas Andrews m. Rebecca Charity 20 Apr. 1791). p. 75

28 June 1808. John CHARITY and Mason Charity, dau. of Mary Blizzard who consents. Sur. Peter Blizzard. (Probably her mother and stepfather.) Married by Rev. James Warren, Methodist. p. 77

27 May 1806. Shadrak CHARITY and Ariana Stephens, dau. of Lucy Stephens who consents. Sur. Major Debrix. Wit. Thomas Peter and William Parker. The groom is also called Sherod Charity in the bond. p. 71

25 April 1791. Squire CHARITY and Lucy Elliott. Sur. Henry Charity. Married 26 April by Rev. Samuel Butler, Rector of Southwark Parish, Episcopal Church. p. 32

13 March 1793. Sterling CHARITY and Elizabeth Jones. Sur. Davis Charity. Wit. Sampson Walden. Married 14 March by Rev. Nathaniel Berriman, Deacon in the Methodist Church. p. 36

27 December 1787. Wilson CHARITY and Susanna Monroe. Sur. William Walden. p. 22

9 February 1796. Wilson CHARITY and Clary Charity. Sur. Sampson Grantham. p. 43

27 January 1810. Edward T. CHARLES and Martha Collier. Sur. James Edwards. Wit. Peter Carrell. Married 1 February by Rev. Nathaniel Berriman, Methodist. p. 82

25 January 1814. Kemp CHARLES and Susanna Carrell. Martha Carrell, guardian of Susanna consents for her. Sur. Edward T. Charles. Wit. John Carrell and James Edwards. Married 29 January by Rev. Nathaniel Berriman, Methodist. p. 94

20 December 1824. Thomas CHARLES and Martha Kee Edwards. Sur. William Edwards. Married 23 December by Rev. Isaiah Harris, Elder in the Methodist Church. p. 130

24 December 1821. James CHEATHAM and Susan S. Rae, dau. of William Wray who consents and is surety. p. 121

12 May 1823. John CHEATHAM and Ann King, dau. of Philip King who consents and is surety. p. 125

25 October 1824. Joseph CHEATHAM and Nancy Blessingham. Sur.
Nicholas Jewell. p. 129

1 January 1824. Archibald CLARK and Elizabeth Gwaltney. Sur.
Willis Clark. Wit. B.C. Bell. p. 128

9 January 1782. James CLARK and Rebecca Bage. Sur. Thomas
Bage. p. 9

12 November 1790. James CLARK and Mary Watkins. Sur. William
Cryer. Wit. M. Smith and Thomas Respes. Married 14 November
by Rev. Samuel Butler, Rector of Southwark Parish, Episcopal
Church. p. 30

21 July 1825. James S. CLARK and Virginia H.L. Maynard. Sur.
Wilie Davis. Wit. Walter S. Booth. p. 132

27 May 1806. John CLARK and Hannah Hargrave. Sur. Benjamin
.Hargrave. p. 71

23 December 1824. Robertson C. CLARK and Wilmouth D. Bennett.
Sur. James Dashiell. p. 130

14 November 1785. William CLARK and Mary Bristow. Married by
Rev. Henry John Burgess, Rector of Southwark Parish, Episcopal
Church. This bond is in Southampton dated 14 Nov. Sur.
William Atkinson. Wit. Benjamin Brock. (Knorr: Southampton
p. 27) Ministers' Returns p. 207

27 February 1794. Benjamin CLARKE and Mary Gray "of age".
Sur. Dolphin Davis. Wit. Nˢ H. Thompson. Married 2 March by
Rev. Nathaniel Berriman, Deacon in the Methodist Church, who
says Clark. p. 38

10 April 1815. Capt. Edward CLARKE and Susan Smith. Sur.
James Clinch. Married 13 April by Rev. James Warren, Methodist.
p. 97

12 December 1792. James CLARKE and Penelope Davis. Sur. Moody
Collier. Married 13 December by Rev. Samuel Butler, Rector
of Southwark Parish, Episcopal Church. p. 35

24 July 1798. James S. CLARKE and Mary Judkins. Sur. Peter
Hamlin. p. 51

20 September 1800. James CLARKE and Nancy Gray. Sur. Langley
C. Wills. Married by Rev. Nathaniel Berriman, Methodist. p. 57

1 October 1791. Jesse CLARKE and Judith Foster. Sur. Thomas
Coggin. p. 33

8 January 1821. Eldridge CLARY and Eliza Jemm. Married by
Rev. Beverly Booth, Baptist Minister. Ministers' Returns p. 234

5 January 1813. Thomas CLARY and Peggy Jones. Sur. John Holloway. Married by Rev. John Gwaltney. p. 91

7 June 1797. Richard CLAYTON and Hannah Richards "property of Henry Moring" who is surety. Wit. Archibald Davis. These are colored people. Married 8 June by Rev. Samuel Butler, Rector of Southwark Parish, Episcopal Church. p. 47

29 December 1777. William CLINCH, Jr. and Rebekah Thompson. Sur. Henry Gilbert. Wit. William Thompson. p. 5

20 February 1786. William CLINCH and Sarah Collier. Sur. William Maget. Married 23 February by Rev. Henry John Burgess, Rector of Southwark Parish, Episcopal Church. p. 18

28 August 1793. Archibald COCKE and Mary T. Crafford. Sur. Thomas Marriott. Married 5 September by Rev. Samuel Butler, Rector of Southwark Parish, Episcopal Church. p. 37

29 November 1787. Benjamin COCKE and Ann Moring, dau. of Benjamin Moring, deceased. Sur. Henry Moring. p. 22

24 November 1817. David COCKE, Jr. and Polly Emery, dau. of David Emery who consents and is surety. p. 106

23 September 1815. Henry M. COCKE and Elizabeth C. Smith. Sur. William Cocke, Jr. Wit. William Smith. p. 98

19 April 1787. James COCKE and Sarah Davis, dau. of Nathan Davis, deceased. Sur. Benjamin Cocke. p. 20

24 November 1794. John Poythress COCKE and Elizabeth Peter. Sur. Thomas Peter. p. 39

24 March 1819. John F. COCKE and Mary S. Lucas. Sur. Stephen Lucas. p. 112

12 December 1810. Richard H. COCKE and Ann Hunt Adams. Sur. Thomas Walke. p. 84

14 June 1824. Richard COCKE and Isabella Ballentine. Sur. William E. B. Ruffin. p. 129

6 April 1791. Robert COCKE and Martha Ruffin Newsum. Francis Ruffin, guardian of Martha consents for her. Sur. Richard Cocke, Jr. Wit. Benjamin Cocke and John Newsum. Married 12 May by Rev. Samuel Butler, Rector of Southwark Parish, Episcopal Church who says Newsom. p. 32

22 December 1789. Thomas COCKE and Polly Berryman. Sur.
Nathaniel Berryman. Married 27 December by Rev. Samuel Butler,
Rector of Southwark Parish, Episcopal Church, who says Cocks
and Berriman. p. 28

28 December 1819. Thomas H. COCKE and Rebecca Richards "of
lawful age". Sur. Pleasant Sheffield, Married 2 January 1820
by Rev. Beverly Booth, Baptist. p. 116

18 November 1788. Walter COCKE and Ann Harrison. Sur. Henry
Harrison. Wit. Carter Bassett Harrison. p. 24

28 September 1815. Henry M. COCKES and Elizabeth E. Smith.
Married by Rev. Nathaniel Berriman, Methodist. Ministers'
Returns p. 228

14 October 1820. Henry M. COCKES and Mary Ann Hart, dau. of
Rebecca Hart. Sur. John N. Carrell. Wit. William Cocks.
Married 23 November by Rev. Benjamin Devaney, Methodist. p. 117

5 July 1816. Henry T. COCKES and Eliza Bailey, dau. of Henry
Bailey, who consents. Sur. Miles Burgess. Wit. Robert H.
Cocks. p. 101

26 April 1803. Thomas COCKES and Elizabeth Wren, dau. of
Thomas Wren who consents and is surety. Married by Rev. Nathaniel
Berriman, Methodist, who says Wrenn. p. 64

24 February 1817. William COCKES, Jr. and Mary R. Cockes.
Sur. John Cockes. Married 17 March by Rev. Nathaniel Berriman,
Methodist. p. 104

26 September 1825. Albert B. COCKS and Mary Ann Hart. Sur.
Hartwell P. Hart. Married 29 September by Rev. John Engles,
Baptist. p. 133

2 September 1824. Benjamin COCKS and Mary Bishop. Sur. John
Faulcon. Wit. Samuel Booth and William R. Bishop. Married by
Rev. Beverly Booth, Baptist. p. 129

26 December 1780. Jesse COCKS and Rebecca Kee, widow. Sur.
John Judkins. Wit. J.S. Young. p. 8

21 August 1813. Jesse COCKS and Susan Smith "21 years of age".
Sur. John Cocks. Wit. Nathaniel Smith and Mary D. Smith.
Married by Rev. Nathaniel Berriman, Methodist. p. 92

9 March 1789. John COCKS and Elizabeth E. Moring. Sur.
William Cocke. p. 25

13 December 1824. John E. COCKS and Jane D. Warren, dau. of
Drury P. Warren who consents. Sur. Nicholas Warren. John
son of John Cocks, Sr. p. 130

8 October 1822. Robert H. COCKS and Lucinda Andrews. Sur.
Jonathan Ellis. Wit. Polly C. Bailey. p. 122

20 December 1815. Samuel COCKS and Susan Pyland, dau. of
Thomas P. Pyland. Sur. James Pyland. Married 21 December by
Rev. Nathaniel Berriman, Methodist. p. 99

18 February 1782. William COCKS and Sarah Moring. Sur. Henry
Moring. p. 10

30 August 1808. John COFER and Peggy Pulley. Sur. Edwin Delk.
p. 77

8 November 1790. Moody COFER and Martha Gwaltney. Sur.
Zachariah Phillips. p. 30

28 January 1797. Samuel COFER and Ann Gwaltney, dau. of James
and Sarah Gwaltney who consent. Sur. William Cornwell.
Married 9 February by Rev. Nathaniel Berriman, Methodist. p. 47

23 December 1789. Henry COKER and Sarah Hargrave. Sur. John
Wilson. p. 28

26 November 1774. John COLE and Elizabeth Burt. Sur. William
Burt. p. 3

5 May 1806. Archibald COLLIER and Rebecca Clinch. Sur. William
Spratley. Married 8 May by Rev. Nathaniel Berriman, Methodist.
p. 71

30 January 1778. Benjamin COLLIER and Patty Cryer. Sur.
Nicholas Cryer. p. 5

27 February 1800. Benjamin COLLIER and Nancy Rae. James Rae
Consents for Nancy; no relationship stated. Sur. John Rae.
Wit. Lucy Rae. p. 56

28 January 1812. George C. COLLIER and Polly Cheatham, dau. of
James Cheatham who consents. Sur. John Cheatham. Married 8
February by Rev. James Hill. p. 87

24 May 1819. George C. COLLIER and Polly Ellis. Sur. Thomas
Binns Ellis. Wit. Thomas Ellis. p. 113

1 June 1789. Howell COLLIER and Susanna Grantham. Sur. William
Grantham. p. 26

24 July 1804. John COLLIER and Martha Burgess. Sur. John
Justiss. p. 67

17 December 1808. John COLLIER Jr. and Mary Flowers. Sur.
Joseph Williamson. p. 78

23 January 1787. Moody COLLIER and Mary Clinch. Sur. William Clinch. p. 20

27 May 1794. Moody COLLIER and Elizabeth Mary Holt. Sur. William Clinch, Jr. Married 29 May by Rev. Nathaniel Berriman, Deacon in the Methodist Church. p. 38

22 June 1779. Stephen COLLIER and Viney Hobbs, dau. of Robert Hobbs who consents. Sur. Joseph Cheatham. Wit. Francis Young. p. 7

22 July 1806. Stephen COLLIER and Fanny S. Grantham, born 10 June 1785, dau. of Stephen Grantham. Henry Dewell gives affidavit as to Fanny's age. Sur. Miles Burgess. Wit. James Warren, Caty Warren and Robert C. Maynard. p. 72

31 January 1825. Stephen COLLIER and Ann E. Cary. Sur. Augustine Bailey. Married 3 February by Rev. Isaiah Harris, Elder in the Methodist Church. p. 131

24 November 1800. Robert COLQUHOUN and Claramond Peter. Sur. John P. Cocke. p. 57

26 March 1782. John COMAN and Lucy Boazman. Sur. Stephen Sorsby. p. 10

29 August 1815. Foster COOK and Martha Johnson. Sur. Beverly Booth. p. 98

17 July 1775. Henry COOK and Betty Lucas. Sur. John Jarratt. p. 4

17 December 1821. Caleb COOPER and Nancy Carsley. Sur. Colin Cooper. p. 121

11 February 1791. Frederick COOPER and Betsy Dewell. Sur. Thomas Dewell. Married 24 February by Rev. Samuel Butler, Rector of Southwark Parish, Episcopal Church. p. 31

20 July 1798. Frederick COOPER and Sarah Rogers. Sur. Benjamin Ellis. Married by Rev. James Warren, Methodist Minister. p. 51

11 December 1789. William CORNWELL and Mary Brown. Sur. David Long. p. 27

20 August 1808. William CORNWELL and Polly Presson. Sur. Samuel Davis. p. 77

22 December 1819. John S. COTWELL and Martha Stewart, dau. of Jesse Stewart who consents. Sur. George Clary. Wit. Elizabeth Stewart. Married 23 December by Rev. Beverly Booth, Baptist. p. 115

19 May 1777. Carter CRAFFORD, Jr. and Sarah Marriott, dau. of Elizabeth Marriott who consents. Sur. Josiah Wilson. Wit. Sally Washington and William Marriott. p. 4

8 April 1780. Henry CRAFFORD and Jane White. Sur. John White. p. 8

4 March 1809. Henry CRAWLEY and Diana Maddera. Sur. Nathaniel Warren. Wit. Prissy Chapman and Samuel Chapman. Married 9 March by Rev. Nathaniel Berriman, Methodist. p. 79.

20 May 1802. John CREWS and Elizabeth Davidson "25 years of age" dau. of Martha Davidson. Sur. Richard Gwaltney. Married by Rev. John Gwaltney. p. 61

17 December 1821. Joshua CRITTENDEN and Ann C. Bell, dau. of Samuel Bell, deceased. Sur. William Randolph. p. 121

13 October 1812. Robert CRITTENDEN and Susan S. Ellis, dau. of Samuel Ellis who consents. Sur. William Edwards. Married 15 October by Rev. Nathaniel Berriman, Methodist. p. 90

25 December 1777. Samuel CROCKER and Ann Holleman "of age", dau. of Arthur Holleman who consents. Sur. Belah Willeford. p. 5

13 December 1788. William CROCKER and Elizabeth Wilson. Sur. William Wilson. p. 24

8 November 1809. John Crafford CRUMP and Mary B. Wilson. Sur. Samuel Wilson. Married 9 November by Rev. Nathaniel Berriman, Methodist. p. 81

19 September 1784. Richard CRUMP and May Crafford. Sur. William Boyce. Richard Crump of Williamsburg. p. 13

4 May 1784. William CRYER and Elizabeth Watkins. Sur. John Barlte, Jr. Wit. Thomas Spratley. p. 13

20 December 1816. William CRYER and Sarah West. Sur. William E. Frazier. Wit. John Bartle and Meriam H. Bilbro. Married 21 December by Rev. Nathaniel Berriman, Methodist. p. 103

28 July 1812. David CYPRESS and Elizabeth Walden. Sur. David Sebrell. Wit. Sillar Walden. Married 6 August by Rev. James Hill. p. 89

26 January 1818. James CYPRESS and Rebecca Bird. Sur. John Charity. p. 107

30 December 1785. William CYPRUSS and Rebecca Walden, dau. of William Walden who consents. Sur. Peter James. p. 17

2 July 1819. Thomas DAVIDSON and Martha Gwaltney. Sur. Sampson Clark. p. 114

23 February 1818. David DAVIES and Charlotte Edwards. Sur. Mark Davies. Wit. James R. Bell. p. 108

25 October 1824. Mark DAVIES and Charlotte Davies. Sur. Jonathan Ellis. Wit. Sarah Bell. p. 130

10 August 1796. Allen DAVIS and Peggy Lane. Sur. Freeman Ward. p. 44

23 October 1815. Allen DAVIS and Elizabeth Moore. Sur. Edwin Epps. Married by Rev. Nathaniel Berriman, Methodist. p. 98

18 December 1787. Archibald DAVIS and Ann Sorsby. Sur. Stephen Sorsby. p. 22

26 April 1791. Archibald DAVIS and Elizabeth Sorsby. Sur. Richard Ellis. p. 32

14 February 1803. Archibald DAVIS and Margaret Gilbert. Sur. John Judkins. Married 17 February by Rev. Nathaniel Berriman, Methodist. p. 63

28 October 1822. Burley DAVIS and Elizabeth Sheffield. Sur. John Johnson. p. 122

12 January 1811. David DAVIS and Lucy Davis. Sur. Samuel Davis. Married by Rev. John Gwaltney. p. 84

23 August 1796. Edwin DAVIS and Nancy Price. Sur. William Carter. Married 1 September by Rev. Nathaniel Berriman, Methodist Minister. p. 45

15 September 1802. James DAVIS and Sally Lane "of lawful age". Sur. John Davis. Wit. James Exum. Married 16 September by Rev. Nathaniel Berriman, Methodist. p. 61

23 January 1790. John DAVIS and Ann Gray, widow of John Gray. Sur. Dolphin Davis. p. 28

22 September 1801. John DAVIS and Elizabeth Thompson. Sur. William Mitchell. Wit. Frederick Warren and Davy Davis. Married 10 October by Rev. Nathaniel Berriman, Methodist. p. 59

24 May 1803. John DAVIS and Sally Lane. Sur. Batts Lane. John Davis son of Hannah Davis. Married 2 June by Rev. Nathaniel Berriman, Methodist. p. 64

27 April 1804. John DAVIS and Rebecca Gwaltney "of lawful age".
Sur. William Adams. Wit. Priscilla Maddera. Married 28 April
by Rev. Nathaniel Berriman, Methodist. p. 67

2 May 1807. Littleberry DAVIS and Elizabeth Porter. Sur.
Richard Carter. Wit. Shadrach Carter. p. 74

11 August 1805. Nathaniel DAVIS and Sally Hart Judkins "of
full age", dau. of Jesse Judkins. Sur. Joseph Warren. Wit.
Nancy Hol-oway. Married 19 August by Rev. Nathaniel Berriman,
Methodist. p. 70

1 July 1797. Robert DAVIS and Susanna Beverley. Sur. Archibald
Davis. p. 48

2 September 1808. Samuel DAVIS and Winnefred Thompson. Sur.
Willis Thompson. p. 77

27 December 1796. William DAVIS and Sarah Emery, dau. of Ruth
Emery, who consents. Sur. James Davis. Wit. Elizabeth Emery.
Married 29 December by Rev. Nathaniel Berriman, Methodist
Minister. p. 46

28 May 1800. William M. DAVIS and Jinsy Bailey. Sur. William
Bailey, Sr. Married 31 May by Rev. Samuel Butler, Rector of
Southwark Parish, Episcopal Church. p. 56

26 December 1809. William DAVIS and Cherry Davis. Sur.
Samuel Davis. Married by Rev. John Gwaltney. p. 81

4 February 1812. Capt. Bartholomew DAWES and Charity Padget.
Sur. Thomas Purkins. Married 9 February by Rev. Nathaniel
Berriman, Methodist, who says Daws and Padgett. p. 87

25 December 1802. David DEBRIX and Nancy Scott. Sur. William
Scott. Married 26 December by Rev. James Warren, Methodist
Minister. p. 62

18 March 1814. Major DEBRIX and Polly Walden "24 years of age".
Sur. Nicholas Scott. Wit. Howell Collier. Married by Rev. -
James Warren, Methodist. p. 94

30 December 1800. Moses DEBRIX and Anne Charity, dau. of
Sarah Charity, who consents. Sur. Davis Charity. Wit. Lucresy
Burgess. Married by Rev. James Warren, Methodist Minister. p. 58

21 January 1817. Richard DEBRIX and Anna Peters, dau. of Jesse
Peters, who consents and is surety. p. 103

21 January 1810. Edwin DELK and Rebecca Young Spratley. Sur.
Littleberry Delk. Wit. Sally Spratley. Married 15 February
by Rev. Nathaniel Berriman, Methodist. p. 82

23 April 1790. James DELK and Martha Bell, dau. of Robert Bell, who consents and is surety. p. 29

19 December 1815. James DELK and Susan Kee. Sur. Jesse Carter. Married by Rev. John Gwaltney. p. 99

31 December 1778. Moreland DELK and Unity Holleman. Sur. Joseph Holleman, Jr. p. 6

23 April 1811. William DELK and Elizabeth Taylor. Sur. Martha Delk. p. 85

21 December 1813. William DELK and Polly White "both over 21 years of age". Sur. James White. Married by Rev. John Gwaltney. p. 93

2 April 1816. Caleb DEWELL and Pegga H. Dewell. Sur. Miles Burgess. Wit. Zachariah Dewell. p. 101

20 November 1788. Drewry DEWELL and Elizabeth Jordan, dau. of William Jordan, who consents and is surety. p. 24

16 December 1802. Henry DEWELL and Elizabeth Putney. Sur. Archibald Milby. Wit. James Bailey. p. 62

27 June 1780. James DEWELL and Hannah Stewart, dau. of John Stewart, who consents. Sur. Joseph Cheatham. Wit. James Kee. p. 8

15 April 1785. Jesse DEWELL and Ann Sledge. Sur. Archer Moody. Wit. Josiah Gray and Silva Clary. p. 15

4 August 1825. Richard DEWELL and Elizabeth A.N. Thompson, dau. of Francis Thompson who consents. Sur. Nicholas Dewell. Wit. Susannah Thompson and John E. Thompson. Married 29 September by Rev. Beverly Booth, Baptist. p. 133

12 May 1823. Thomas B. DEWELL and Nancy Collier Bailey. Sur. John Cheatham. Wit. Henry Bailey. Married 15 May by Rev. Isaiah Harris, Elder in the Methodist Church. p. 125

22 March 1788. William DEWELL and Rebecca Avriss, dau. of John Averiss who consents. Sur. Henry Dewell. Wit. Stephen Sorsby and Nathaniel Beddingfield. p. 23

20 November 1822. William DEWELL and Nancy Roney "both of lawful age". Sur. Matthew Booth. p. 123

20 August 1800. Wyatt DEWELL and Rhoda Justiss. Sur. Edmund Carseley. Wit. Patsea Dewell. Married 21 August by Rev. James Warren, Methodist Minister. p. 57

9 September 1796. Francis DILLARD and Susan Southall "of age".
Sur. John Nicholas Burt. p. 45

21 December 1772. David DONMAN and Amy Davis Bouth. Sur.
Henry Brown. p. 1

12 November 1807. James DOUGLAS and Mary Moring, dau. of Sarah
Moring, who consents. Sur. William Moring. Married by Rev.
Nathaniel Berriman, Methodist. p. 75

21 May 1801. John DOUGLASS and Margaret Moore. Sur. Benjamin
Bell, Jr. Married 23 May by Rev. Nathaniel Berriman, Methodist.
p. 59

18 December 1799. James DOWDEN and Dorcas Partin. Sur. Henry
Dewell. p. 54

17 June 1824. James B. DOWDEN and Elizabeth Bishop "of lawful
age." Sur. James C. Partin. Married 22 June by Rev. Beverly
Booth, Baptist. p. 129

1 November 1785. Thomas DOWDEN and Esther Bishop, dau. of
John Bishop, who consents. Sur. William Bishop. Married 5
November by Rev. Henry John Burges, Rector of Southwark Parish,
Episcopal Church. p. 17

11 February 1801. John DREW and Betsy Pyland. Sur. Langley
Crafford Wills. Wit. Robert McIntosh, Jr. Married 12 February
by Rev. Samuel Butler, Rector of Southwark Parish, Episcopal
Church. p. 59

25 June 1807. John DREW and Elizabeth Edwards. Sur. James
Edwards. Wit. John Mallicote. Married by Rev. Nathaniel
Berriman, Methodist. p. 74

27 November 1810. Richard DREW, Jr. and Mary Carter. Sur.
Richard Carter. p. 83

7 May 1821. William B. DREW and Sally B. Bryant. Consent of
Henry and Rebecca Johnston for Sally. (Henry Johnston m.
Rebecca Bryant 24 Nov. 1812). Sur. William S. Lucas. Wit.
Joel Bryant. Married 10 May by Rev. James Warren, Methodist.
p. 119

19 December 1791. James DREWRY and Sarah Coggin. Sur.
Micajah Coggin. Married 20 December by Rev. Samuel Butler,
Rector of Southwark Parish, Episcopal Church. p. 33

9 January 1777. Richard DREWRY and Mary Champeon. Sur. William
Delk. p. 4

20 October 1817. Thomas Watkins DRURY and Eliza C. Newsum "21 years of age", dau. of Mary Newsum, who consents. James D. Edwards, guardian of Thomas, is surety. Wit. Alexander A. Newsum and Susanna Slade. p. 106

26 April 1779. Edward DUDLEY and Ann Holt. Sur. James Simmons. Wit. John Holt. p. 7

14 January 1778. Archibald DUNLOP and Mrs. Nancy I'Anson. Sur. William Nelson. p. 5

25 March 1791. Archibald DUNLOP and Susanna Buchanan. Sur. James Kee. Married by Rev. Samuel Butler, Rector of Southwark Parish, Episcopal Church, who says Buchannan. p. 31

14 December 1816. Jacob EATON and Anicha Blow. Free persons of color. Sur. Henry Charity. Married 15 December by Rev. Nathaniel Berriman, Methodist. p. 102

3 January 1792. John EDMONDSON and Lucy Cocke. Sur. Thomas Marriott. Married 5 January by Rev. Samuel Butler, Rector of Southwark Parish, Episcopal Church. p. 34

23 November 1785. Charles EDMUNDS and Elizabeth Edwards, dau. of Micajah Edwards, deceased. Sur. Benjamin Lewis. Married 24 November by Rev. Henry John Burges, Rector of Southwark Parish, Episcopal Church. p. 17

31 October 1782. Thomas EDMUNDS and Martha Short. Sur. Thomas Blunt. p. 10

22 June 1818. William EDMUNDS and Mary H. Cocke. Sur. Richard Cocke. p. 109

3 December 1803. Edwin EDWARDS and Polly Harriss. Sur. James Edwards. Married 15 December by Rev. Nathaniel Berriman, Methodist. p. 65

29 September 1807. Herbert EDWARDS and Laodocia Edwards. Sur. Benjamin Ward. Married 10 October by Rev. Nathaniel Berriman, Methodist. p. 75

24 November 1798. James EDWARDS and Elizabeth Collier. Samuel Carrell consents for Elizabeth; no relationship stated. Sur. William Cryer. Wit. Joseph Ramey. Married by Rev. James Warren, Methodist Minister. p. 51

23 December 1800. James EDWARDS, Jr. and Nancy Meed "21 years of age". Sur. William Carter. Married by Rev. Nathaniel Berriman, Methodist Minister, who says Mead. p. 58

17 April 1811. Capt. James Davis EDWARDS and Phoebe Bell
"21 years of age", sister of Fielden Bell who consents and is
surety. Wit. William P. Graves and Henry Bell. Married by
Rev. Nathaniel Berriman, Methodist. p. 85

14 March 1809. Joel EDWARDS and Sally Kee, dau. of Robert Kee
who consents. Sur. William B. Kee. Married 16 March by Rev.
Nathaniel Berriman, Methodist. p. 79

12 February 1787. Jesse EDWARDS and Mary Gwaltney. Sur. Joseph
Gwaltney. p. 20

4 February 1793. John EDWARDS and Martha Bennett. Sur. William
Bennett. Married 28 February by Rev. Nathaniel Berriman,
Deacon in the Methodist Church. p. 36

13 May 1814. Lee EDWARDS and Lilly Edwards "both 21 years of
age". Sur. Benjamin Edwards. Wit. Thomas Talley. Married
14 May by Rev. Nathaniel Berriman, Methodist. p. 95

28 February 1820. Nelson EDWARDS and Ann Seeds. Sur. Willis
D. Warren. p. 116

27 March 1812. Patrick EDWARDS and Priscilla Hart "both of
lawful age". Jesse Bennett gives affidavit as to age of both.
Sur. Joel Holloway. Married 31 March by Rev. Nathaniel Berriman,
Methodist. p. 88

26 August 1822. Richard H. EDWARDS and Mary H. Edmunds. Sur.
Richard Cocke. p. 122

29 May 1817. Samuel EDWARDS, Jr. and Sarah Edwards "21 years
of age". Sur. Rowland Edwards. Wit. Thomas Edwards. Married
by Rev. Josiah Bidgood, Deacon in the Methodist Church. p. 105

17 September 1796. Thomas D. EDWARDS and Charlotte Long,
22 years of age. Consent of Hannah Long "grandmother who raised
her". Sur. John Moring, Jr. Married 1 October by Rev. Nathaniel
Berrmian, Methodist. p. 45

2 February 1785. Thomas Swan EDWARDS and Neomi Crocker, of
age. Sur. William Wills. Wit. Josiah Gray and Benjamin
Walker. p. 14

8 September 1803. Thomas EDWARDS and Martha Ruffin, dau. of
Francis Ruffin, deceased. Sur. Caufield Seward. p. 64

8 July 1784. William EDWARDS and Martha Edwards, dau. of
William Philip Edwards, who consents and is surety. Wit.
Thomas Bland, Jr. p. 13

8 November 1797. William EDWARDS and Martha Edwards "better than 22 years of age". Sur. Lewis Edwards. Wit. Samuel Wilson and Henry Edwards. Married 12 November by Rev. Nathaniel Berriman, Methodist. p. 49

14 May 1800. William EDWARDS and Mary Bishop. Sur. Amos Gwaltney. Married 15 May by Rev. Nathaniel Berriman, Methodist. p. 56

6 February 1809. William T. EDWARDS and Cherry Price "of lawful age". Sur. Edwin Davis. Married 16 February by Rev. Nathaniel Berriman, Methodist, who says <u>Charity</u> Price. p. 79

19 February 1791. Robert ELDRIDGE and Mary Irby. Sur. Lemuel Cocke. p. 31

23 August 1819. Benjamin W. ELLINSWORTH and Elizabeth Gray. Sur. Frederick Gray. Married by Rev. Nathaniel Berriman, Methodist, who says <u>Ellingsworth</u>. p. 114

19 September 1798. Robert ELLIOTT and Nancy Debereux. Sur. John Debereux. Married 20 September by Rev. Samuel Butler, Rector of Southwark Parish, Episcopal Church. p. 51

26 July 1819. Archibald ELLIS and Sarah A. Velvin. Sur. John Velvin. p. 114

10 September 1780. Benjamin ELLIS and Martha Caseley. Sur. Michael Caseley. p. 8

4 May 1791. Benjamin ELLIS and Sarah Jones. Sur. Frederick Cooper. Wit. William Ellis. Married 13 May by Rev. Samuel Butler, Rector of Southwark Parish, Episcopal Church. p. 32

22 November 1819. Boling ELLIS and Elizabeth Ann Velvin. Sur. John Velvin. Married 30 December by Rev. Beverly Booth, Baptist. p. 115

28 July 1823. James W. ELLIS and Cassandra Maynard. Sur. George G. Collier. p. 126

17 December 1782. John ELLIS and Lucy Price, widow of Randolph Price, nee Lucy Hamlin. Sur. William Hamlin. p. 11

28 September 1785. Joseph ELLIS and Susanna Atkins. Sur. Benjamin Bilbro. Wit. Josiah Gray. Married by Rev. Henry John Burges, Rector of Southwark Parish, Episcopal Church. Return dated 2 March 1786. p. 17

28 March 1809. Joseph ELLIS and Pollener Bailey. Sur. Aaron Bailey. Free negroes. p. 80

4 February 1783. Richard ELLIS and Jane Binns. Sur. William Clinch. Wit. David Cocke. p. 11

23 December 1783. Thomas ELLIS and Ann Carrell. Sur. Archibald Davis. p. 12

5 March 1801. Thomas ELLIS and Sarah Sharp. Sur. James White, Jr. p. 59

5 April 1803. Thomas ELLIS, Sr. and Sarah Clinch. Sur. John Judkins. Wit. Elizabeth Ellis. Married 9 April by Rev. Nathaniel Berriman, Methodist. p. 64

30 October 1788. Charles EMERY and Rebecca Moody. Sur. James Smith. p. 24

28 November 1795. Charles EMERY and Dorothy Lanier. Sur. John Bartle, Jr. Wit. Elizabeth Bartel. Married 1 December by Rev. Nathaniel Berriman, Methodist Minister. p. 42

25 July 1809. Charles EMERY and Nancy Clarke. Sur. John Scammell. Wit. Henry Gray. Married 27 July by Rev. Nathaniel Berriman, Methodist. p. 80

5 February 1818. Clabon EMERY and Anny Emery. Married by Rev. James Warren, Methodist. Ministers' Returns p. 230

2 January 1808. Drewry EMERY and Sally Emery. Sur. David Cocke. Wit. David Johnson and Lucretia Emery. p. 76

27 April 1813. Drewry EMERY and Catharine Emery. Sur. James Emery. Wit. John F. Kilby. Married 2 May by Rev. James Warren, Methodist. p. 92

9 August 1822. Holleman EMERY and Frances Emery, dau. of Howell Emery. Sur. Clayton Emery. p. 122

29 March 1809. Kiah EMERY and Frances Johnson. Sur. Thomas Johnson. p. 80

3 March 1813. Lemuel EMERY and Elizabeth Emery. Sur. David Emery. Wit. John F. Kilby. p. 91

5 September 1811. Moody EMERY and Nancy J. James "of lawful age". Sur. Thomas Maddera. Married 9 September by Rev. Nathaniel Berriman, Methodist. p. 86

11 August 1815. Moody EMERY and Susanna James "21 years of age", dau. of Sylviah James. Sur. Peter T. Spratley. Wit. Edwin James. Married 12 August by Rev. Nathaniel Berriman, Methodist. p. 97

29 December 1803. Nathan EMERY and Keziah Emery. Sur. Peyton Hobbs. Married 1 January 1804 by Beverly Booth, Baptist Minister. p. 65

27 September 1785. Peyton EMERY and Lucretia Emery. Sur. John Emery. Wit. Josiah Gray. Married 1 October by Rev. Henry John Burges, Rector of Southwark Parish, Episcopal Church. p. 16

1 December 1817. Peyton EMERY and Mrs. Rhody Hite. Sur. Simmons Hite. Wit. Peyton Hobbs. p. 107

26 March 1816. Edwin EPPS and Harriott Edwards. Sur. Benjamin Edwards. Married by Rev. Nathaniel Berriman, Methodist. p. 101

23 November 1815. Maxey ETHERIDGE and Ann S. Warren. Sur. Joseph Cary. Married by Rev. Nathaniel Berriman, Methodist. p. 98

13 April 1786. Benjamin EVANS and Mary Ellis. Married by Rev. Henry John Burges, Rector of Southwark Parish, Episcopal Church. This bond is in Sussex dated 6 April 1786. Mary dau. of William Ellis. Sur. Waller Bailey. Wit. Robert Bailey. (Knorr: Sussex p. 25) Ministers' Returns p. 208

14 December 1779. William EVANS and Rebecca Drew. Sur. William Hart. p. 7

7 January 1796. John FARRELL and Susanna Stewart. Sur. Frederick Savidge. Married 8 January by Rev. Samuel Butler, Rector of Southwark Parish, Episcopal Church. p. 43

17 June 1773. Jacob FAULCON and Ann Spratley, dau. of John Spratley, Gent., deceased. Sur. William Spratley. Wit. Thomas Fivash. p. 2

31 May 1802. John FAULCON and Jane Faulcon. Sur. James Davis Edwards. p. 61

14 May 1807. John FAULCON, Jr. and Mary Ann Faulcon. Sur. John FAULCON. p. 74

27 July 1813. John FAULCON and Mary Kennon Cocke. Sur. Nicholas Faulcon. p. 92

27 April 1818. John FAULCON and Martha Edwards. Sur. Richard H. Edwards. Wit. Samuel Rowell. Married by Rev. Richard Dobbs. p. 108

8 December 1792. Nicholas FAULCON, Jr. and Sally Cocke, dau. of John H. Cocke, deceased. Sur. Jacob Faulcon. Married 10 December by Rev. Samuel Butler, Rector of Southwark Parish, Episcopal Church. p. 35

6 September 1798. John FENN and Sarah Watkins. Sur. John Watkins, Sr. p. 51

9 January 1822. William H. FINCH and Pamala Blunt, dau. of Thomas Blunt, deceased. Sur. Richard H. Edwards. p. 121

27 December 1824. John R. FITCHETT and Nancy J. Bell. Sur. Dawson Warren. Wit. Nicholas T. Davies and Mark Davies. Married 1 January 1825 by Rev. Nicholas Presson. p. 131

18 September 1794. Randolph FITCHETT and Rebecca Bell, dau. of Michael Bell, deceased. Benjamin Bell, guardian of Rebecca, consents for her and is surety. p. 38

17 December 1802. Joseph FIVEASH and Polley Harriss. Sur. Thomas Harriss. Married 23 December by Rev. Jesse Holleman, Sr. p. 62

22 September 1813. Thomas FLAKE and Lucy Phillips, dau. of Zachariah Phillips who consents. Sur. Thomas P. Gwaltney. Wit. John B. Lane. p. 92

11 July 1797. James FLETCHER and Sally Harri (illegible). Sur. Francis Ruffin. p. 48

29 July 1782. Thomas FLETCHER and Jane Coupland. Sur. Thomas Peters. p. 10

22 February 1784. Sterling FOSTER and Ann Marks, dau. of John Marks, who consents. Sur. Henry Marks. Sterling Foster of Southampton County. p. 15

18 November 1801. William FOSTER and Mary Coman "21 years of age". James A. Bradley gives affidavit as to Mary's age. Sur. Langley Crafford Wills. Married by Rev. Nathaniel Berriman, Methodist. p. 59

28 December 1825. Benjamin FRANCIS and Elizabeth Taylor, dau. of Aaron Taylor who consents. Henry Francis makes affidavit as to Benjamin being 21 years of age. Sur. Sampson Banks. Wit. Henry Francis and Right Walden. p. 134

15 March 1822. Henry FRANCIS and Polly Taylor. Sur. John Williams, Sr. Wit. John Williams and Henry Charrity. Henry Frances of Isle of Wight County. Married 16 March by Rev. John Blunt, Deacon in the Methodist Church. p. 121

22 December 1817. James D. FRAZIER and Elizabeth Seward. Sur.
John Carrell. Wit. William Seward and Nancy Seward. Married
25 December by Rev. Nathaniel Berriman, Sr., Methodist. p. 107

18 June 1783. William FRAZIER and Sally Carrell "of age", dau.
of Thomas Carrell who consents. Sur. Charles Judkins. p. 12

24 February 1807. William E. FRAZIER and Elizabeth H. Baugh
"of lawful age". Sur. John Bartle, Jr. Wit. Nancy Cryer. p. 73

11 April 1818. William E. FRAZIER and Susanna Slade. Sur.
Thomas W. Drewry. See William Phrasure. p. 108

13 July 1791. Abraham FREELAND and Mary Ann Barker. Sur.
William Rae. Married 14 July by Rev. Samuel Butler, Rector of
Southwark Parish, Episcopal Church. p. 32

23 April 1821. Archibald FREELAND and Martha W. Emery. Sur.
Carter Marks. p. 119

30 November 1811. Charles FREEMAN and Sally Andrews, widow.
Sur. Josiah Freeman. Married 4 December by Rev. Drewry Lane.
p. 86

23 March 1807. David FULKS and Sarah Charity, dau. of Judith
Charity who consents. Sur. David Debrix. Wit. Howell Collier
and Hamblin Cypress. p. 73

13 December 1777. George GARDNER and Lucy Warren. Sur. Robert
Ward. p. 5

24 August 1816. Archer GEORGE and Emma Bailey, a free woman
of color. Sur. Carter French. Wit. Richard Wrenn and John
Holt. Married 3 September by Rev. Nathaniel Berriman, Methodist.
p. 101

18 January 1785. William GILBERT and Charity Smith, dau. of
Mary Smith who consents. Sur. John Lane. Wit. Josiah Gray
and Henry Lane. William Gilbert of Sussex County. p. 14

20 December 1798. William GILCHRIST and Lurana Debereux. Sur.
Samuel Thompson. Married by Rev. James Warren, Methodist
Minister, who says Debereaux. p. 52

25 April 1809. William GILCHRIST and Leziah Fagan "of lawful
age". Sur. William Parker. Wit. William Maynard. Married
30 April by Rev. James Hill. p. 80

10 January 1817. Samuel GLOVER and Sarah Persons, dau. of
Ann Persons who consents. Sur. James White. Wit. Burwell
Persons. Married 11 January by Rev. Josiah Bidgood, Deacon
in the Methodist Church. p. 103

2 August 1785. George GODBY and Ann Edwards, dau. of Thomas Edwards who consents. Sur. Richard Edwards. Wit. Josiah Gray. p. 16

30 October 1815. Henry H. GOFFIGAN and Sally Harwood. Sur. William Scammell. Married 2 November by Rev. Nathaniel Berriman, Methodist. p. 98

26 December 1805. Abednega GOODRICH and Clary Price. Sur. Meshack Goodrich. Married by Rev. Nathaniel Berriman, Methodist, who says Clary <u>Pierce</u>. p. 70

7 February 1804. Bell GOODRICH and Averille Holleman, dau. of Joseph Holleman who consents. Sur. John Presson. Wit. George Holleman. Married by Rev. Jesse Holleman, Sr. who says <u>Averilla</u>. p. 66

27 December 1803. James GOODRICH and Frances Edwards. Sur. Benjamin Goodrich. Married 29 December by Rev. Nathaniel Berriman, Methodist. p. 65

25 February 1803. Shadrick GOODRICH and Dolly Holt. Sur. Thomas Goodrich. Married 29 February by Rev. Nathaniel Berriman, Methodist. p. 63

20 December 1803. Thomas GOODRICH and Hearty Gray, dau. of Henry Gray who consents and is surety. Married 26 December by Rev. Nathaniel Berriman, Methodist. p. 65

12 June 1797. John GOODSON and Elizabeth Randolph Bell. Sur. Benjamin Bell. p. 47

6 January 1809. Wilson GOODSON and Sarah Smith "of lawful age". Sur. Thomas Goodrich. Wit. Anne Nelson. Married 7 January by Rev. Nathaniel Berriman, Methodist. p. 79

8 January 1773. William GOOSLEY and Ludwell Harrison. Sur. Nathaniel Burwell. Nathaniel Harrison consents for Ludwell; no relationship stated. p. 2

29 December 1808. Joshua GRAMMON and Sally Solloman "of lawful age". N. Marks, guardian of Sally, consents for her. Sur. David Cocke. p. 78

16 February 1796. Lewis GRANTHAM and Lucy Austin. Sur. Henry Bishop. p. 44

25 June 1793. Sampson GRANTHAM and Catharine Bedingfield. Sur. Samuel Carrell. Married 13 July by Rev. Samuel Butler, Rector of Southwark Parish, Episcopal Church. p. 36

25 May 1809. Sampson GRANTHAM and Sally Bailey. Sur. William
Bailey, Sr. Married 27 May by Rev. Nathaniel Berriman, Methodist.
p. 80

22 April 1817. Sampson GRANTHAM and Elizabeth Willeford.
Sur. Moses Bishop. Wit. Miles Burgess. p. 104

23 July 1793. Thomas GRANTHAM and Rebecca Thomas. Sur.
Sampson Grantham. Married 10 August by Rev. Samuel Butler,
Rector of Southwark Parish, Episcopal Church. p. 36

22 January 1787. William GRANTHAM and Peggy Justiss. Sur.
John Tillott. p. 22

2 November 1789. William GRANTHAM and Nancy Bishop, dau. of
Joshua Bishop who consents and is surety. Married 19 November
by Rev. Samuel Butler, Rector of Southwark Parish, Episcopal
Church. p. 27

4 June 1805. Charles H. GRAVES and Patsy Browne, dau. of
Benjamin E. Browne. Sur. Reubin Butler. p. 69

24 November 1823. Fielding GRAY and Lucy E. Clark. Sur.
Micajah Holt. p. 127

7 August 1787. Henry GRAY and Elizabeth Brown, dau. of Richard
Dixon Brown, who consents. Sur. Dixon Brown. p. 21

28 April 1817. James GRAY and Louisa W. Mallecote. Sur.
Francis Holt. p. 105

24 September 1821. Joseph M. GRAY and Coney Thomas. Sur.
Matthew Thomas. Married 22 October by Rev. Joseph Bidgood,
Deacon in the Methodist Church, who says Conney. p. 120

16 August 1788. Josiah GRAY and Elizabeth West. Sur. John
Mallicott. p. 23

17 November 1777. Abraham GREEN and Elizabeth Browne, dau. of
Henry Browne, Gentleman, deceased. Sur. Henry Browne of
Southampton County. William Browne consents that Elizabeth
Browne of Surry marry Abraham Green of Amelia. Wit. Lemman
Still and Benjamin Browne. p. 5

27 February 1817. William GRIMES and Elizabeth Warren, dau.
of James Warren. Sur. John A. Warren. p. 104

2 December 1815. Henry L. GUTHRIE and Sally E. Smith "of
lawful age". Sur. Philip Smith. Wit. Jonathan Ellis and
Rebekah B. Clark. Married 5 December by Rev. Nathaniel
Berriman, Methodist. p. 99

27 February 1819. Henry GUTHRIE and Mary Scammell. Married
by Rev. Nathaniel Berriman, Methodist. Ministers' Returns.
p. 231

7 October 1786. Amos GWALTNEY and Lucretia Maddera. Sur.
David Long. p. 19

16 November 1804. Edmund GWALTNEY and Nancy Carter "of lawful
age", dau. of William Carter. Sur. Richard Gwaltney. Married
by Rev. John Gwaltney. p. 68

25 July 1786. James GWALTNEY and Elizabeth Holleman. Sur.
Joseph Holleman. p. 19

27 September 1796. James GWALTNEY and Polly (Mary) Davis, dau.
of James Davis who consents. Sur. Joel Thompson. Married by
Rev. Nathaniel Berriman, Methodist. Returns dated 10 November.
(James son of James and Elizabeth Gwaltney of Isle of Wight
County.) p. 45

25 January 1803. John GWALTNEY and Winnefred Davis. Sur.
James Davis Edwards. Wit. Samuel Davis. Married 3 February
by Rev. Jesse Holleman, Sr. p. 63

8 November 1810. John GWALTNEY and Mary Jemima Cofer. Sur.
Richard Gwaltney. James Gwaltney of <u>Isle of Wight County</u>,
guardian of Mary, consents for her. p. 83

10 August 1819. John GWALTNEY and Elizabeth Bailey. Sur.
Josiah Turner. Married 11 August by Rev. Nathaniel Berriman,
Methodist. p. 114

18 May 1815. Laurence GWALTNEY and Ann Gwaltney, dau. of
Martha Gwaltney, who consents. Sur. James Gwaltney. p. 97

28 December 1818. Nathaniel GWALTNEY and Rebecca Gwaltney.
Sur. Richard Holt. p. 111

26 October 1808. Sampson GWALTNEY and Rebecca Holt. Sur.
James Holt. p. 78

25 February 1811. Thomas P. GWALTNEY and Elizabeth Warren.
Sur. Benjamin C. Bell. Benjamin Bell, guardian of Elizabeth,
consents for her. Married 26 February by Rev. Nathaniel
Berriman, Methodist. p. 84

18 February 1804. Willis GWALTNEY and Elizabeth Edwards, dau.
of Lewis Edwards. Sur. Richard Gwaltney. Wit. Sampson
Gwaltney. Married by Rev. John Gwaltney. p. 66

27 June 1797. Peter HAMLIN and Dolly Evans. Sur. Edwin D.
Hart. Married 13 July by Rev. Samuel Butler, Rector of
Southwark Parish, Episcopal Church. p. 48

20 February 1775. William HAMLIN and Rebecca Faulcon. Sur.
Nicholas Faulcon, Jr. p. 4

12 August 1817. William HAMLIN and Mary Ann Jemm. Sur. Joshua
Savedge. Wit. Ann T. Jemm. p. 105

27 February 1798. James HANCOCK and Elizabeth Gibbons. Sur.
Isham Inman. Married 17 March by Rev. Drewry Lane. p. 50

2 December 1794. John HANCOCK and Miriam Hargrave. Sur.
Charles Holdsworth. Married 4 December by Rev. Drewry Lane.
p. 39

22 June 1808. John HARDIE and Susanna Moring, dau. of Sarah
Moring, who consents. Sur. Philip King. Married 23 June by
Rev. Nathaniel Berriman, Methodist. p. 77

13 February 1785. Thomas HARDY and Priscilla Binns. Sur.
Robert Hunnicutt. Wit. Josiah Gray. p. 15

15 July 1785. John HARDYMAN and Hannah Harrison. Sur.
William Collins. Wit. Josiah Gray. Married 16 July by Rev.
Henry John Burges, Rector of Southwark Parish, Episcopal
Church. Another record says <u>Susanna</u>. p. 16

20 April 1802. Thomas M. HARE and Catharine Wallace. Sur.
Samuel Butler. Wit. Martha R. Butler. Married 21 April by
Rev. Samuel Butler, Rector of Southwark Parish, Episcopal Church.
p. 60

15 September 1819. Benjamin HARGRAVE and Sally Clark. Sur.
William Hargrave. Wit. John E. Clark. p. 115

28 January 1822. Benjamin HARGRAVE and Mary Stewart, dau. of
Jesse Stewart, who consents. Sur. John E. Clark. Wit. William
S. Pleasants. Married by Rev. Burwell Barrett, Sr. Return
dated 7 March. p. 121

7 August 1824. Benjamin HARGRAVE and Martha Edwards. Sur.
Richard C. Jones. p. 129

25 May 1815. Emanuel HARGRAVE and Martha Roberts, free people
of color. Emanuel of Isle of Wight County. Sur. Robert
Hargrave. Wit. Drewry P. Warren. p. 97

12 February 1791. Herman HARGRAVE and Dianna Cofer. Sur.
Thomas Cofer. p. 31

25 March 1816. Lemuel HARGRAVE and Patsey Womble. Sur.
Richard H.L. Bailey. p. 100

18 December 1798. Pleasant HARGRAVE and Elizabeth Hargrave.
Sur. John Hargrave. Married 3 January 1799 by Rev. Drewry Lane.
p. 52

21 December 1819. Robertson M. HARGRAVE and Ann H. Savedge.
Sur. James Jones. Married by Rev. James Warren, Methodist.
p. 115

24 May 1819. Thomas HARGRAVE and Lucy Rix. Sur. Ruffin Bailey.
Wit. Micajah Holt. p. 113

1 January 1816. William HARGRAVE and Rebecca Briggs. Sur.
Daniel Pond. Married by Rev. John Gwaltney. p. 100

27 January 1789. Hansel HARPER and Elizabeth Rose. Sur.
John Rose. p. 25

24 February 1817. Benjamin C. HARRIS and Margaret C. White.
Sur. Edwin Edwards. p. 104

10 January 1788. Hamlin HARRIS and Margaret Belches. Sur.
Francis Harris. p. 22

24 February 1823. Hardy HARRIS and Sally Pleasant, dau. of
Burwell Pleasant. Sur. Isham Inman. Married 27 February by
Rev. Williamson Hoskins Pittman. p. 124

14 July 1823. Rev. Isaiah HARRIS and Frances Love. Sur.
John Cocks. Wit. J. White and Hollaman Whitmore. p. 126

1 January 1824. John HARRIS and Nancy Cocks. Sur. Richard
Booth. Wit. William J. Pulley. Married 3 February by Rev.
Burwell Barrett. p. 128

3 March 1795. Travis HARRIS and Mary Lee Campbell. Sur. John
Newsum. Married by Rev. Samuel Butler, Rector of Southwark
Parish, Episcopal Church. Return dated 30 April. p. 40

5 February 1798. Hardy HARRISS and Elizabeth Holleman. Sur.
Thomas Bevan. Married 13 February by Rev. Nathaniel Berriman,
Methodist. p. 50

9 April 1795. Randolph HARRISS and Elizabeth W. Lane. Sur.
Henry Crafford. Married 11 April by Rev. Nathaniel Berriman,
Methodist Minister. p. 40

28 March 1796. Thomas HARRISS and Polly Bevan. Sur. Hardy
Harriss. p. 44

17 May 1801. Benjamin HARRISON and Mary Ann Harrison. Married
by Rev. Samuel Butler, Rector of Southwark Parish, Episcopal
Church. Ministers' Returns p. 218

15 January 1787. Carter Bassett HARRISON and Mary Howell Allen,
dau. of William Allen, who consents. Sur. John Watkins. p. 20

26 January 1796. Coleman HARRISON and Sarah Sorsby. Sur.
James Kee. Married 4 February by Rev. Nathaniel Berriman,
Methodist. p. 43

13 December 1785. Henry HARRISON and Polly Stark Cocke. Sur.
Walter Cocke. Married 15 December by Rev. Henry John Burges,
Rector of Southwark Parish, Episcopal Church. He says Mary
Stark Cocke. p. 17

27 August 1792. James William HARRISON and Mary Ann Kee.
Sur. James Key. Married 1 September by Rev. Samuel Butler,
Rector of Southwark Parish, Episcopal Church. p. 34

11 October 1797. James HARRISON and Elizabeth Barker "of age",
dau. of John Barker, deceased. J(ames?) Kee makes affidavit
as to Elizabeth's age and is surety. Wit. Thomas Kee. Married
21 October by Rev. Samuel Butler, Rector of Southwark Parish,
Episcopal Church. p. 48

18 November 1794. Pleasant HARRISON and Jane Lucas. Sur.
William Simmons. p. 39

28 March 1803. Robert HARRISON and Charlotte Pretlow. Joseph
G. Bailey, guardian of Charlotte, consents for her. Sur.
Walter Blunt. p. 63

22 November 1824. Samuel HARRISON and Mary Almond. Sur.
Benjamin Jones. Wit. Timothy Atkinson. Samuel Harrison of
Isle of Wight County. Married by Josiah Bidgood, Deacon in
the Methodist Church. p. 130

24 April 1820. Shadrack M. HARRISON and Ann Bailey. Sur.
Thomas Dewell. Married 27 April by Rev. James Warren,
Methodist. p. 116

10 March 1818. Theodorick P. HARRISON and Susan Bailey. Sur.
John Bartle. Married 11 March by Rev. James Warren, Methodist.
p. 108

20 February 1796. William HARRISON and Elizabeth Clarke.
Sur. Sampson Harrison. p. 44

30 January 1821. Hamlin HART and Eliza Parr. Sur. Richard
Parr. Married 1 February by Rev. Williamson Hoskins Pittman.
p. 118

28 April 1817. Henry S. HART and Peggy Rogers. Sur. Benjamin
B. Atkinson. Groom's name given also as Henry T. Hart. p. 105

7 September 1795. Jesse HART and Rebecca Thompson, dau. of
Joel and Sarah Thompson who consent. Sur. John Williams.
Wit. John Bell and N^s H. Thompson. Married 10 September by
Rev. Nathaniel Berriman, Methodist Minister. p. 41

41

8 April 1823. Jesse H. HART and Mary Ann Smith. Married by Rev. Isaiah Harris, Elder in the Methodist Church. Ministers' Returns p. 234

9 November 1779. Joseph HART and Hanah Bailey. Sur. William Bailey, Jr. p. 7

1 October 1787. Lemuel HART and Mary Pretlow. Sur. Samuel Pretlow. p. 21

13 January 1816. Robert HART and Polly Holloway. Sur. Hamlin Carter. Married by Rev. John Gwaltney. p. 100

17 January 1820. Ruffin HART and Mary M. Rispess. Sur. Christopher Rispess. Married 28 January by Rev. James Warren, Methodist. p. 116

9 December 1785. William HART and Sarah Drewry. Sur. David Long. Wit. Richard Drewry. Married 15 December by Rev. Henry John Burges, Rector of Southwark Parish, Episcopal Church. p. 17

12 July 1790. William Ruffin HART and Elizabeth Gray. Sur. William Wilson. p. 29

20 November 1820. William HART and Martha Savedge. Sur. Robert Hart. Married 21 November by Rev. Nathaniel Berriman, Methodist. p. 117

22 November 1808. Benjamin HARWOOD and Sally McIntosh. Sur. Robert McIntosh, Sr. Married 9 December by Rev. Nathaniel Berriman, Methodist. p. 78

26 February 1812. John HARWOOD and Charlotte Holt "21 years of age". James Simpson gives affidavit as to Charlotte's age. Sur. John Mallicote. Married 27 February by Rev. Nathaniel Berriman, Methodist. p. 88

20 December 1771. Major HARWOOD and Lucy Watson, dau. of James Watson, who consents. See Harwood Major. p. 1

25 December 1809. Edwin HASTY and Polly Thompson. Sur. Joel Wall. Married by Rev. John Gwaltney. p. 81

2 December 1801. Jacob HAWK and Eliza Warren. Married by Rev. Nathaniel Berriman, Methodist Minister. Ministers' Returns p. 217

24 September 1776. Thomas HAYNES and Mrs. Catherine Allen Bradley. Sur. Allen Cocke. Thomas Haynes of Halifax County, North Carolina. Bride's name also spelled Bradby. p. 4

9 July 1821. John HAYWOOD and Hannah Williams, dau. of James Williams, who consents and is surety. Wit. William Holloway. John is son of William Hawood. Note: John Haywood "of age and free born". Married 23 July by Rev. James Warren, Methodist. p. 120

23 December 1806. Moze Congress HEMMINGS and Elizabeth Richards. Sur. Jonathan Richards. Wit. Peter Thomas Spratley. p. 73

7 December 1810. Bartholomew D. HENLEY and Martha B. Cocke. Sur. William Edwards. p. 84

24 February 1817. Bartholomew D. HENLEY and Martha Ann Cocke. Sur. Richard H. Cocke. Married 27 February by Rev. Nathaniel Berriman, Methodist. p. 104

21 May 1798. James HIGHT and Anne Coggin. Sur. Charles Emery. p. 50

23 December 1819. Exum HILL and Elizabeth Bailey. Sur. Moses Pretlow. Wit. James A. Bailey. p. 115

7 July 1818. Ivy HILL and Nancy Eaton. Sur. Archer George. Married 9 July by Rev. Jesse Holleman, Sr. Ivy and Nancy are free negroes. p. 109

5 May 1819. Robert S. HINTON and Rebecca B. Carsley. Sur. Augustine Carsley. p. 113

26 October 1802. Nicholas HITE and Ann Grantham, widow of William Grantham, nee Ann (Nancy) Bishop, dau. of Joshua Bishop. Sur. David Bishop. Wit. Joshua Bishop. p. 61

23 December 1801. Simmons HITE and Amy Hickman "22 years of age". Sur. James Bishop. Married by Rev. James Warren, Methodist Minister. p. 60

10 September 1810. William HIX and Mildred Johnson "of lawful age". Sur. Miles Johnson. Wit. Peter Johnson and Harmon Bishop. p. 83

7 December 1816. Edwin HOBBS and Ann Rebecca Lucas. Sur. Stephen Lucas. p. 102

15 June 1778. Robert HOBBS and Lucy Waller. Sur. Capt. John Davis. p. 6

15 February 1792. James HODGES and Jane Brown. Sur. William Mitchell. p. 34

15 December 1820. Braxton HOLDCROFT and Sarah T. Parker. Sur. Philip Burt. p. 118

2 February 1818. Archibald HOLDSWORTH and Nancy Rogers. Sur. Benjamin Rogers. Married 4 February by Rev. Nicholas Presson, who says Macy Rogers. p. 107

25 March 1783. Benjamin HOLDSWORTH and -------- ---------
Sur. Swan Lunsford. Wit. John Judkins. p. 11

26 July 1819. Robert HOLDSWORTH and Susan Sharp. Sur. Robert
H. Watkins. Wit. James Briggs. Married 11 August by Rev.
Williamson Haskins Pittman. p. 114

6 October 1787. Christopher HOLLEMAN and Elizabeth Inman.
Sur. Benjamin Bell. p. 21

13 March 1809. Jonathan HOLLEMAN and Nancy Cornwell, dau. of
William Cornwell, who consents. Sur. Thomas P. Gwaltney. p. 79

28 April 1778. Joseph HOLLEMAN, Jr. and Sarah Gwaltney, dau.
of Thomas Gwaltney, who consents. Sur. William Nelson. Wit.
Solomon Holmes. p. 6

11 October 1811. Willis HOLLEMAN and Ann Lane. Sur. Joel
Wall. Wit. Joseph Lane. p. 86

9 July 1816. John HOLLINGSWORTH and Frances Bishop, dau. of
William Bishop, Sr. and Winne Bishop. Sur. William Bishop.
Wit. John Bishop. p. 101

11 March 1814. Elijah HOLLOWAY and Sally Phillips "both 21
years of age". Sur. Willis Thompson. Wit. John T. Kilby.
Married 17 March by Rev. Nathaniel Berriman, Methodist. p. 94

17 February 1823. Isham HOLLOWAY and Keziah, alias Keziah
Bowser, free people of color, dau. of Ann Bowser. Sur. Willis
White. Wit. Nancy Bowser. Isham about 24 years of age. p. 124

25 March 1816. James HOLLOWAY and Sarah Bennett, dau. of Jesse
Bennett, who consents and is surety. Married by Rev. John
Gwaltney. p. 100

25 March 1800. Jesse HOLLOWAY and Sarah Warren, dau. of Ann
Warren, who consents. Sur. Mark Holloway. Wit. Jesse Little.
Married 27 March by Rev. Nathaniel Berriman, Methodist. p. 56

13 January 1810. Joel HOLLOWAY and Polly Hart, dau. of Sarah
Hart, who consents. Sur. Jesse Bennett. Married 16 January
by Rev. Nathaniel Berriman, Methodist. p. 82

26 February 1816. John HOLLOWAY and Eliza M. Lane. Sur.
William Cocks, Sr. p. 100

15 August 1785. Lazarus HOLLOWAY and Sarah Brown. Sur. John
Pettway. p. 16

9 December 1796. Mark HOLLOWAY and Lucy Warren, dau. of Arthur and Ann Warren, who consent. Sur. William Pleasant. Married 10 December by Rev. Nathaniel Berriman, Methodist. p. 45

2 September 1805. Silas HOLLOWAY and Ann Hunnicutt Thompson "21 years of age". Sur. Nicholas H. Thompson. Married 4 September by Rev. Nathaniel Berriman, Methodist. p. 70

17 March 1821. Thomas HOLLOWAY, Jr. and Sally Rowell, dau. of Samuel Rowell, Sr., who consents. Sur. Stephen Ellis. Married 18 March by Rev. Nathaniel Berriman, Methodist. p. 119

22 October 1791. William HOLLOWAY and Sally Bennett. Sur. William Slade, Jr. Wit. William Bennett and James P. Bell. William Holloway son of Lazarus Holloway. p. 33

30 April 1804. William HOLLOWAY and Winefred Holloman, dau. of Joseph Holleman, who consents. Wit. George Holleman. Married by Rev. Jesse Holleman, Sr., who says Holleway and Holleman. p. 67

22 December 1796. Edward Salter HOLT and Fanny Andrews. Sur. John Andrews. Married 24 December by Rev. Nathaniel Berriman, Methodist Minister. p. 46

25 June 1799. Francis HOLT and Mary Scammell. Sur. William Scammell. Wit. William Holt. Married 4 July by Rev. Nathaniel Berriman, Methodist. p. 53

18 November 1802. Francis HOLT and Elizabeth Mallicote, widow of John Mallicote. Sur. Richard Pierce. Married 20 November by Rev. Nathaniel Berriman, Methodist. p. 61

23 November 1813. Henry HOLT and Charity Judkins. Sur. Micajah Holt. Married by Rev. John Gwaltney, who says Cherry Judkins. p. 92

1 December 1781. Capt. James HOLT and Martha Cocke "of lawful age". Sur. John Stewart. p. 9

17 January 1783. James HOLT and Rebecca Edwards, dau. of William Philip Edwards, who consents. Sur. Archer Holt. Wit. David Cocke. p. 11

20 July 1808. James HOLT and Elizabeth E. Holt. Sur. Robert McIntosh. Married 21 July by Rev. Nathaniel Berriman, Methodist. p. 77

30 September 1815. James HOLT and Sally W. Bennett, dau. of James Bennett, who consents and is surety. Married by Rev. Nathaniel Berriman, Methodist. p. 98

3 February 1821.   John HOLT and Polly W. Hancock, dau. of
Elizabeth W. Hancock who consents.   Sur. John Bevan.   Married
21 March by Rev. Williamson Hoskins Pittman.   p. 119

14 December 1822.   Josiah HOLT and Nancy M. Andrews.   Sur. John
Maddera.   Wit. John Underhill.   p. 123

20 March 1815.   Micajah HOLT and Nancy Lane.   Sur. Joseph Lane.
Married 23 March by Rev. Nathaniel Berriman, Methodist.   p. 97

5 December 1816.   Micajah HOLT and Martha Thompson.   Sur.
Lemuel Hargrave.   Married by Rev. John Gwaltney.   p. 102

23 August 1803.   Michael HOLT and Polly Judkins, dau. of
Samuel Judkins, who consents and is surety.   Married by Rev.
John Gwaltney.   p. 64

26 December 1825.   Nicholas HOLT and Susanna Carrell.   Sur.
Albert B. Cocke.   Wit. Jacob Barns.   p. 134

15 May 1800. Rowland HOLT and Ann Faulcon.   Sur. Jacob Faulcon.
Married by Rev. Samuel Butler, Rector of Southwark Parish,
Episcopal Church.   p. 56

18 January 1804.   Rowland HOLT and Ann Binns Hunnicutt, dau.
of John Hunnicutt.   Sur. William Butts.   Married 19 January
by Rev. Nathaniel Berriman, Methodist.   p. 66

21 December 1791.   Thomas HOLT and Lucy Riggan, dau. of Jesse
Riggan, who consents.   Sur. Joseph Thorp.   Wit. Thomas Riggan.
Married 22 December by Rev. Samuel Butler, Rector of Southwark
Parish, Episcopal Church.   p. 34

13 July 1779.   William HOLT and Mildred Hargrove.   Sur. Arthur
Warren.   p. 7

20 January 1823.   John P. HOPKINS and Patsey Bailey, dau. of
Henry Bailey, who consents and is surety.   Married 22 January
by Rev. Isaiah Harris, Elder in the Methodist Church.   p. 123

10 November 1818.   Stephen A. HOPKINS and Marinda Seaver.   Sur.
Norman L. Seaver.   Wit. Winney E. Seaver.   Married 11 November
by Rev. Nathaniel Berriman, Methodist.   p. 110

19 December 1791.   William HOPKINS and Sarah Pettway.   Sur.
John Pettway.   Married 22 December by Rev. Samuel Butler,
Rector of Southwark Parish, Episcopal Church.   p. 33

23 March 1779.   Henry HOWARD and Betty Wilbrow.   Sur. Thomas
Howard.   Wit. Francis Young.   p. 7

24 May 1785. Henry HOWARD, Jr. and Sarah Bilbro, dau. of John Bilbro, who consents. Sur. Nathaniel Sebrell. Betty Howard, guardian of Henry Howard, Jr., consents for him. p. 16

27 November 1804. Henry J. HOWARD and Sarah Booth, dau. of Beverley Booth, Gentleman, who consents. Sur. Robert Booth. Wit. Matthew Booth. p. 68

25 February 1783. Augustine HUNNICUTT and Bramley Hart. Sur. Rodwell Delk. p. 11

22 January 1823. Augustine W. HUNNICUT and Eliza Shelly. Sur. Merit Shelly. Married 23 January by Rev. John Blunt, Deacon in the Methodist Church. p. 124

6 December 1813. Caufield HUNNICUTT and Mary Hunnicutt, widow. Sur. Willis Thompson. Wit. Williamson Talley. Married 7 December by Rev. Nathaniel Berriman, Methodist. p. 93

15 February 1779. Hartwell HUNNICUTT and Mary Seward. Sur. Britain Seward. James Seward consents to daughter's marriage. p. 6

27 January 1778. John HUNNICUTT and Martha Binns. Sur. Henry Crafford. John, son of Robert Hunnicutt who consents. Eliza Binns, guardian of Martha, consents for her. No relationship stated. p. 5

3 December 1814. John HUNNICUTT, Sr. and Lucy Thornton. Sur. John Bartle. Married 10 December by Rev. Nathaniel Berriman, Methodist. p. 95

29 September 1817. John HUNNICUTT, Jr. and Hannah Moody. Sur. Blanks Moody. Married 6 October by Rev. Nathaniel Berriman, Methodist. p. 106

24 June 1783. Robert HUNNICUTT and Elizabeth Binns, dau. of Thomas Binns, deceased. Sur. Nicholas Faulcon, Jr. p. 12

30 October 1806. Robert B. HUNNICUTT and Elizabeth Barham, "upwards of 21 years of age", dau. of Joseph Barham who is surety. Wit. Joseph Barham, Jr. and James Barham. Married by Rev. Nathaniel Berriman, Methodist. p. 72

11 February 1807. Thomas HUNNICUTT and Mary Clinch, dau. of William Clinch, Jr., deceased. Thomas Ellis, guardian of Mary, consents for her. Sur. John Hunnicutt. Wit. Nathaniel Berriman, Sr. Married by Rev. Nathaniel Berriman, Methodist. p. 73

23 June 1805. William HUNNICUTT and Elizabeth Smalley, dau. of John Smalley, deceased. Sur. John Hunnicutt. Married 6 August by Rev. Nathaniel Berriman, Methodist. p. 69

16 January 1808. James HUNTER and Nancy Cofer. Sur. Thomas P. Gwaltney. p. 76

15 December 1788. John I'ANSON and Martha Wright Mackie. Sur. Andrew Mackie, Jr. p. 24

11 October 1783. Thomas I'ANSON and Mary Mackie, dau. of Andrew Mackie, who consents. Sur. Andrew Mackie, Jr. p. 12

8 March 1824. John INGRAM and Elizabeth Pyland, dau. of Benjamin Pyland, who consents. Sur. Albridgton Seward. p. 128

28 December 1792. William INGRAM and Sally Green. Sur. John Williams. Married 1 January 1793 by Rev. Nathaniel Berriman, Deacon in the Methodist Church. p. 35

10 September 1808. Henry INMAN and Rebecca Judkins "21 years of age". Sur. John Pond. p. 77

8 September 1779. Isham INMAN and Mary Gibbons. Sur. William Evans. p. 7

23 April 1800. Isham INMAN and Hannah Pond. Sur. Daniel Pond. p. 56

26 February 1805. Isham INMAN and Lucy Harris. Sur. Thomas Harris. p. 69

25 August 1823. Isham INMAN and Elizabeth Judkins. Sur. John Lane. p. 126

26 January 1825. John D. INMAN and Elizabeth Andrews, dau. of Henry Andrews, deceased. Sur. Isham Inman. Married 27 January by Rev. Nicholas Presson. p. 131

4 January 1781. William IRBY and Jane Edmonds. Sur. William Edwards. William Blunt, guardian of Jane, consents for her. Wit. Lemuel Cocke and Nathan Jones. p. 9

4 December 1815. Elijah JACKSON and Rebekah James "of lawful age". Sur. Moody Emery. Married by Rev. John Gwaltney. p. 99

11 June 1817. Edwin JAMES and Mary B. Pyland "upwards of 21 years of age". Sur. Jonathan Ellis. Wit. William Pyland and Thomas P. Pyland. Married 12 June by Rev. Nathaniel Berriman, Sr., Methodist. p. 105

26 July 1819. John JAMES and Rebecca Edwards, dau. of Skelton Edwards, deceased. Sur. Benjamin Edwards. p. 114

11 December 1799. Moland JAMES and Peggy Slade. Sur. Moses Savidge. Married 15 December by Rev. Nathaniel Berriman, Methodist. p. 54

16 January 1809. Mourland JAMES and Charity Warren. Sur. John Lane. Married 19 January by Rev. Nathaniel Berriman, Methodist. p. 79

22 January 1773. John JARRETT and Rebecca Mooring. Sur. John Mooring. p. 2

22 September 1791. Peter JEMM and Ann Judkins Burt. Married by Rev. Samuel Butler, Rector of Southwark Parish, Episcopal Church. See Peter Jenn. Ministers' Returns p. 211

20 September 1791. Peter JENN and Ann J. Burt. Sur. Edward Burt. Wit. John W. Burt. See Peter Jemm. p. 32

23 January 1802. David JOHNS and Polly Scott, dau. of Nicholas Scott. Sur. Drewry Walden. Wit. William Simmons. p. 60

9 February 1818. Reuben JOHNS and Rebecca Walden. Sur. John Walden. Married 10 February by Rev. James Warren, Methodist. p. 107

29 April 1791. Allen JOHNSON and Elizabeth Perry. Sur. David Codke. Married 1 May by Rev. Samuel Butler, Rector of Southwark Parish, Episcopal Church. p. 32

25 May 1814. Andrew JOHNSON and Susanna Riggan. Sur. William Ingram. Wit. John Williams. Married by Rev. Nathaniel Berriman, Methodist. p. 95

30 May 1815. Augustine JOHNSON and Mary Ann Hite. Sur. Miles Johnson. p. 97

25 December 1790. Caesar JOHNSON and Tiller Trusty. Sur. Hercules Trusty. Married by Rev. Samuel Butler, Rector of Southwark Parish, Episcopal Church. p. 30

20 November 1810. Edmund JOHNSON and Lucy Solomon. Sur. Randolph Johnson. Nathaniel Martin of Prince George County, guardian of Lucy, consents for her. p. 84

26 March 1782. Hartwell JOHNSON and Susanna Emery. Sur. Howell Emery. Wit. John Spratley. p. 10

24 November 1812. Henry JOHNSON and Rebecca Bryant. Sur. Thomas Bailey, Jr. Wit. Edward S. Holt. p. 90

4 April 1789. Isaac JOHNSON and Daphney Trusty. Sur. Samuel Trusty. p. 26

10 October 1820. John JOHNSON and Anna Debrix. Sur. Jesse Peters. Married 12 October by Rev. Beverly Booth, Baptist. p. 117

9 March 1816. Levi JOHNSON and Nancy Sheffield, dau. of
Hardiman Sheffield. Sur. James Sheffield. Wit. John Johnson.
p. 100

8 December 1814. Levy JOHNSON and Nancy Emery, dau. of David
Emery, who consents and is surety. Married by Rev. James
Warren, Methodist. p. 95

12 November 1800. Mike JOHNSON and Polly Pilkenton "upward of
21 years of age". Sur. Allen Johnston. p. 57

18 September 1814. Miles JOHNSON and Winefred Wright "21 years
of age". Sur. Micajah Little. Wit. William Spratley. Married
by Rev. Nathaniel Berriman, Methodist, who says Elizabeth
Wright. p. 95

1 February 1786. Moses JOHNSON and Sally Girl. Sur. Hercules
Trusty. Married 18 February by Rev. Henry John Burges, Rector
of Southwark Parish, Episcopal Church. p. 18

25 August 1807. Peter JOHNSON and Betsy Johnson, dau. of
William Johnson, who consents and is surety. p. 75

26 October 1803. Randolph JOHNSON and Anne Sheffield, dau. of
Hardiman Sheffield, who consents and is surety. Married 2
November by Rev. Beverly Booth, Baptist, who says Shuffield.
p. 65

26 August 1822. Reuben JOHNSON and Martha Jones "of lawful
age". Sur. Randolph Johnson. Wit. Silas Marks. p. 122

8 September 1808. Richard JOHNSON and Polly Emery, dau. of
David Emery, who consents and is surety. p. 78

9 October 1824. Travis W. JOHNSON and Priscilla Emery "upwards
of 21 years of age", dau. of David Emery, who consents and
is surety. Married 11 October by Rev. Beverly Booth, Baptist.
p. 129

14 October 1825. Reubin JOHNSTON and Tempeah Marks. Sur.
Daniel Marks. Married 18 October by Rev. Beverly Booth,
Baptist. p. 133

24 December 1807. Edmund JOINER and Charlotte Little. Polly
Jones, guardian of Charlotte, consents for her. Sur. William
Royce. Married by Rev. Nathaniel Berriman, Methodist. p. 75

19 March 1808. Thomas JOINER and Conney Little. Sur. Henry
Gray. Married 26 March by Rev. Nathaniel Berriman, Methodist.
p. 76

26 November 1783. Cadwalder JONES and Mary Pride, dau. of
Halcott Pride, deceased. Sur. Thomas Cocke. p. 12

6 December 1773. Daniel JONES and Susanna Hardy, dau. of
Littleberry Hardy. Sur. William Eaton, Jr. Will Green Munford,
guardian of Susanna, consents for her. Wit. James New and Ann
Munford. p. 2

16 November 1790. David JONES and Frances Barlow. Sur.
James Barlow. p. 30

24 January 1802. David JONES and Polly Scott. Married by Rev.
James Warren, Methodist Minister. Ministers' Returns p. 218

26 February 1805. Edward Salter JONES and Mary Phillips, widow
of William Phillips. Sur. John Davis, Jr. Wit. John Davis.
Married 28 February by Rev. Nathaniel Berriman, Methodist.
p. 69

9 February 1814. Edwin JONES and Susan A. Marriott "21 years
of age". Sur. Richard H. Edwards. Married 17 February by
Rev. Nathaniel Berriman, Methodist. p. 94

20 February 1811. Irby JONES and Rebecca B. Edwards. Sur.
Thomas Edwards. p. 84

-27 April 1795. Isaac JONES and Elizabeth Thomas. Sur. John
Thomas. p. 40

29 October 1792. James JONES and Betsy Salter. Sur. Henry
Crafford. p. 35

8 Sepember 1797. James JONES and Catharine Harris. Sur.
Francis Ruffin. Wit. Ann Faulcon. Married 10 September by
Rev. Samuel Butler, Rector of Southwark Parish, Episcopal
Church. p. 48

1 May 1813. James JONES and Ann Judkins. Sur. Thomas Barham
Adams. Married by Rev. Nathaniel Berriman, Methodist. p. 92

26 October 1818. James JONES and Martha Bishop, dau. of
Harmon Bishop, who consents. Sur. Miles Burgess. Wit. Carter
Marks. p. 110

7 March 1820. James JONES and Martha Barham. Sur. Joseph
Warren. Married by Rev. Nathaniel Berriman, Methodist. p. 116

20 September 1797. Jesse JONES and Mary Little, Sur. Richard
Scammell. Married 24 September by Rev. Nathaniel Berryman,
Methodist. p. 48

28 October 1811. Nicholson JONES and Elizabeth C. Bell, dau.
of James P. Bell, who consents. Sur. Joseph Davis. Married
by Rev. John Gwaltney. p. 86

20 November 1798. Richard JONES and Elizabeth Campbell. Sur.
Colin Campbell. Married 22 November by Rev. Samuel Butler,
Rector of Southwark Parish, Episcopal Church. p. 51

28 December 1822. Richard JONES and Nancy Lane, widow of Joel
Lane. Sur. Howell Simmons. p. 123

2 March 1808.   Robert JONES and Nancy Thomas, dau. of Matthew
Thomas, who consents and is surety.   p. 76

4 November 1816.   Thomas JONES and Margaret Moore.   Married
by Rev. Nathaniel Berriman, Methodist.   Ministers' Returns
p. 228

2 March 1811.   William JONES and Ann Ruffin.   Sur. Richard H.
Edwards.   Married 7 April by Rev. Nathaniel Berriman, Methodist.
p. 85

13 December 1790.   Willis JONES and Lucy Boyce.   Sur. William
Boyce.   p. 30

24 February 1795.   Amos JUDKINS and Lucy Lane.   Sur. John Pyland.
Married 26 February by Rev. Nathaniel Berriman, Methodist
Minister.   p. 40

11 April 1818.   Benjamin JUDKINS and Elizabeth R.P. Pyland.
Sur. Robert Moring.   Married 12 April by Rev. Nathaniel
Berrmian, Sr., Methodist.   p. 108

2 April 1802.   George JUDKINS and Margaret Lucas.   Married by
Rev. Nathaniel Berriman, Methodist.   Ministers' Returns p. 218

4 February 1818.   Henry H. JUDKINS and Mary Lane.   Sur. Banjamin
Judkins.   Married by Rev. Nathaniel Berriman, Sr., Methodist.
p. 107

8 October 1774.   James JUDKINS and Mary Ann Judkins.   Sur.
Samuel Judkins.   p. 3

2 February 1778.   James JUDKINS and Lucy Cockes, dau. of
William Cockes, who consents.   Sur. Jesse Cockes.   p. 6

20 May 1780.   James JUDKINS and Mary Rowell.   Sur. Richard
Rowell.   p. 8

24 January 1792.   James JUDKINS and Elizabeth Andrews.   Sur.
John Andrews.   Married 26 February by Rev. Daniel Southall.
p. 34

29 November 1794.   James JUDKINS and Anna Berriman.   Sur.
Richard Rowell, Jr.   Wit. Sarah Rowell.   Married 30 November
by Rev. Nathaniel Berriman, Methodist Minister, who says Ann.
p. 39

3 March 1817.   James JUDKINS, Jr. and Nancy Rowell "21 years
of age".   Sur. Richard Rowell.   Wit. Thomas Rowell.   Married
28 March by Rev. Nathaniel Berriman, Methodist.   p. 104

22 November 1774.   Jesse JUDKINS and Sally Simmons.   Sur.
Charles Judkins.   p. 3

4 February 1782. Jesse JUDKINS and Mildred Holloway. Sur. Hartwell Edwards. p. 9

25 April 1795. John JUDKINS and Ann Spratley, dau. of John Pettway, who consents. Sur. William Adams. Does this mean step-father? Married by Rev. Nathaniel Berriman, Methodist. p. 40

9 February 1797. John JUDKINS and Rebecca Savidge, dau. of Sarah Savidge, who consents. Sur. Robert Phillips. Wit. Benjamin Barham. Married by Rev. Nathaniel Berriman, Methodist. p. 47

23 June 1817. John W. JUDKINS and Sally R. Berriman. Sur. Joseph Berryman. Married 26 June by Rev. Nathaniel Berriman, Sr., Methodist. p. 105

20 July 1820. John P. JUDKINS and Ann Faulcon Holt. Sur. John N. Spratley. Married by Rev. Nathaniel Berriman, Methodist. p. 117

6 October 1783. Jordan JUDKINS and Sally Warren, dau. of Samuel Warren, deceased. Sur. Mark Judkins. Wit. Thomas Spratley. p. 12

23 November 1785. Joseph JUDKINS and Mary Presson, dau. of John Presson, who consents and is surety. Married 24 November by Rev. Henry John Burges, Rector of Southwark Parish, Episcopal Church. p. 17

30 December 1803. Joseph JUDKINS and Selah Warren. Sur. Samuel Warren. Married 5 January 1804 by Rev. Nathaniel Berriman, Methodist. p. 65

12 December 1825. Joseph P. JUDKINS and Elizabeth Cocks, dau. of John Cocks, who consents. Sur. Wyatt Cocks. Wit. William Cocks. Married 15 December by Rev. Isaiah Harris, Elder in the Methodist Church. p. 133

19 October 1792. Nathaniel JUDKINS and Mary Lane. Sur. William Judkins. p. 35

30 November 1818. Nicholas JUDKINS and Polly Ingram "above the age of 21 years". Nicholas son of Thomas Judkins. Sur. Augustine Wright. Wit. Josiah Turner and John Williams. Married by Rev. Nathaniel Berriman, Methodist. p. 111

14 February 1784. Samuel JUDKINS and Hannah Presson, dau. of John Presson, who consents. Sur. William Judkins. Wit. Thomas Bland, Jr. p. 13

27 December 1796. Thomas JUDKINS and Polly Price. Sur. Thomas Turner. Married 3 January 1797 by Rev. Nathaniel Berriman, Methodist Minister. p. 46

26 March 1819. Thomas JUDKINS and Sarah Wright. Sur. Josiah Turner. Married by Rev. Nathaniel Berriman, Methodist. p. 113

4 April 1789. William JUDKINS and Susanna Moring, dau. of
Benjamin Moring, who consents. Sur. Henry Moring. p. 26

18 August 1812. William JUDKINS and Polly Wright "above the
age of 21". Sur. Josiah Turner. Wit. Austin Wright. Married
20 August by Rev. Nathaniel Berriman, Methodist. p. 89

29 November 1802. William JUSTICE and Nancy Andrews "of
lawful age". Sur. Daniel A. Matthews. p. 61

23 November 1820. William JUDKINS and Rebecca Barham. Sur.
Nathaniel Davis. Wit. Joseph Barham. Married by Rev.
Nathaniel Berriman, Methodist. p. 118

10 April 1797. John JUSTISS and Mary Williford. Sur. James
Willeford. p. 47

23 February 1813. James KEA and Elizabeth Little. Sur.
Thomas Little. See James Kee. p. 91

31 October 1795. Robert KEA and Elizabeth Steward. Sur.
Hartwell Edwards. Married 20 November by Rev. Nathaniel
Berriman, Methodist Minister. p. 41

1 September 1806. William B. KEA and Susanna Holloway, dau.
of Jesse Holloway, who consents. Sur. Silas Holloway. p. 72

22 February 1774. James KEE and Jane Bailey, dau. of Thomas
Bailey, deceased. Mary Bailey, guardian of Jane, consents.
Sur. Etheldred Gray. Wit. Samuel King, Jr. and John Swan. p. 2

-- ------ 1814. James KEE and Elizabeth Little. Married by
Rev. John Gwaltney. Ministers' Returns p. 225

26 January 1773. Samuel KELLO and Margaret Belches, dau. of
Patrick Belches, deceased. Sur. James Belches. p. 2

4 November 1793. Andrew KELSEY and Giley Johnson. Sur.
William Johnston. Married 17 November by Rev. Samuel Butler,
Rector of Southwark Parish, Episcopal Church, who says Gilly.
p. 37

27 March 1819. Andrew KELSEY and Elizabeth Hix. Sur. William
Hix. See Andrew Celsey. p. 113

28 March 1786. Edward KING and Rebecca Judkins. Sur. Thomas
Bailey. Wit. Josiah Gray. Married 30 March by Rev. Henry
John Burges, Rector of Southwark Parish, Episcopal Church.
p. 18

8 April 1825. George W. KING and Ann Rogers. Married by
Rev. Beverly Booth, Baptist. Ministers' Returns p. 237

3 February 1785. Jesse KING and Rebecca Putney. Sur. Michael Smith. Wit. Josiah Gray. p. 14

2 October 1816. Jesse KING and Martha Collier. Sur. Christopher Rispess. Wit. Wiley Davis and Thomas Clinch. Married 3 October by Rev. Nathaniel Berriman, Methodist. p. 101

26 January 1796. Philip KING and Elizabeth Moring. Sur. John Moring. Married 28 January by Rev. Nathaniel Berriman, Methodist. p. 43

26 December 1789. Thomas KING and Lucy Bailey. Sur. Thomas Bailey. Married 30 December by Rev. Samuel Butler, Rector of Southwark Parish, Episcopal Church. p. 28

22 January 1823. Thomas KING and Polly Collier Bailey "of lawful age". Sur. Alexander Bailey. Wit. Joseph Bailey. p. 124

20 November 1823. William KING and Nancy Wright. Sur. John Bennett. Wit. James Bennett. Married by Rev. Isaiah Harris, Elder in the Methodist Church. p. 127

22 January 1824. Wyatt LAIN and Susan Cocks. Married by Rev. Beverly Booth, Baptist. Ministers' Returns p. 237

1 June 1786. John LAMB and Aggy Briggs. Married by Rev. Henry John Burges, Rector of Southwark Parish, Episcopal Church. Ministers' Returns p. 208

22 January 1821. John H.E. LAMB and Polly C. Carsley. Sur. Richard Cocke. Wit. Jonathan Ellis. p. 118

9 November 1797. James Smith LAND and Elizabeth Hart. Married by Rev. Samuel Butler, Rector of Southwark Parish, Episcopal Church. See James S. Lane. Ministers' Returns p. 215

14 September 1811. John LAND and Mary Drew Hart. James S. Lane, guardian of Mary, consents for her. Sur. John Spratley. p. 86

2 May 1797. Batts LANE and Mary Ann Barham. Sur. Joseph Barham. Married by Rev. Nathaniel Berriman, Methodist. p. 47

30 January 1779. Frederick LANE and Becky Thompson. Sur. John Judkins. p. 6

9 October 1797. James S. LANE and Elizabeth Hart. Sur. Carter Nicholas. See James Smith Land. p. 48

24 December 1817. Jesse LANE and Betsey Brown. Sur. Jesse Brown. p. 107

2 August 1794. Joel LANE and Nancy Warren, dau. of Anne Riggan, who consents. Sur. Arthur Warren. Wit. Jesse Warren. Joel Lane, son of Rebecca Moore who consents. Anne Warren m. William Riggan 19 Dec. 1791. Joel probably son of Frederick Lane. Married 14 August by Rev. Nathaniel Berriman, Deacon in the Methodist Church. p. 38

1 January 1799. John LANE and Fanny Holloway. Sur. Nathaniel Judkins. p. 52

8 October 1803. John LANE and Nancy Long, dau. of David Long. Sur. Joel Lane. Wit. Thomas D. Edwards. Married by Rev. Nathaniel Berriman, Methodist. p. 65

1 January 1805. Thomas LANE and Sally Warren. Sur. John Warren, Sr. Married 10 January by Rev. Nathaniel Berriman, Methodist. p. 69

16 December 1785. William LANE and Mary Champion. Sur. Joel Wall. p. 17

30 January 1805. Thomas LASHLEY and Mary Emery "21 years of age", dau. of Howell Emery. Sur. David Emery. Wit. Peter J. Spratley and David Cocke. p. 69

5 March 1785. William LAUGHTON and Helena Reid Nimmo, dau. of Andrew Nimmo, who consents and is surety. p. 15

21 October 1797. Nicholas LAYLOR and Faithy Edwards "21 years of age last June". Sur. Jesse Edwards. Wit. James Laylor. Married by Rev. Nathaniel Berriman, Methodist. p. 49

3 February 1823. Littleberry M. LEE and Lucy Warren, dau. of James Warren, who consents. Sur. John A. Warren. p. 124

21 December 1811. John LEWELLIN and Sally McIntosh Mallicote. Sur. John Mallicote. See John L. Wellin. p. 87

22 October 1822. Edmund LEWELLING and Peggy Mallicote. Sur. Richard Rowell. Wit. John Mallicote, Jr., Betsy Mallicote, Daniel Marrow and John Marrow. Edmund Lewelling born 29 Oct. 1798 son of James Lewelling. Married 31 October by Rev. John Blunt, Deacon in the Methodist Church. p. 123

9 April 1804. William H. LIGHTFOOT and Sarah S. Stewart. Sur. William C. Holt. p. 66

28 December 1800. James LITTLE and Tabitha Portis. Sur. Joseph Davis. Wit. James D. Edwards and Sarah Gwaltney. Married by Rev. Nathaniel Berriman, Methodist. p. 58

26 February 1811. John LITTLE and Nancy Warren "21 years of age". Sur. Thomas Brown. Married 7 March by Rev. Nathaniel Berriman, Methodist. p. 85

10 November 1806. Micajah LITTLE and Ann Wright, widow of Isham Wright. Sur. Richard Carter. p. 72

2 February 1825. Robert LITTLE and Ann Carter. Sur. Hamlin Carter. p. 131

11 December 1786. Samuel LITTLE and Charity Carter, dau. of Mourning Carter (mother) who consents. Sur. Isham Wright. p. 19

23 January 1810. Thomas LITTLE and Susan Carter. Sur. Richard Carter. Married 25 January by Rev. Nathaniel Berriman, Methodist. p. 82

23 January 1816. William LITTLE and Susanna H. Stewart. Sur. Willis D. Warren. Wit. Jack C. Bell. Married 25 January by Rev. Nathaniel Berriman, Methodist. p. 100

15 January 1824. Cary LIVESAY and Rebecca Grantham. Married by Rev. Beverly Booth, Baptist. Ministers' Returns p. 237

11 November 1805. James LOGAN and Lucy Judkins, dau. of John Judkins, deceased. Mary Judkins consents for Lucy; no relationship stated. Sur. Thomas Price. Married 14 November by Rev. Nathaniel Berriman, Methodist. p. 70

23 June 1807. David LONG and Rebecca Williams. James H. Warren, guardian of David Long, consents for him. Sur. John Williams. Wit. William Spratley and Blanks Moody. Married 2 July by Rev. Nathaniel Berriman, Methodist. p. 74

22 May 1820. Thomas LOVESAY and Nancy Stewart. Sur. Caleb Cowper. Wit. Miles Burgess and Miles T. Burgess. Married 23 May by Rev. Beverly Booth, Baptist. p. 116

8 April 1812. Archer LOWERY and Nancy Charity, dau. of Sterling Charity, who consents. Sur. Joseph Roberts. Wit. William Maynard. p. 88

17 June 1783. Christopher LUCAS and Elfibet Dawson, dau. of George Dawson, deceased. Sur. William Bailey. p. 12

24 December 1793. Christopher LUCAS and Mary Sorsby. Sur. Stephen Sorsby. p. 37

24 March 1779. James LUCAS and Mary Lucas. Sur. John Lucas. p. 7

28 February 1786. James LUCAS and Keziah Bunkley. Sur. Sampson Grantham. Married 4 March by Rev. Henry John Burges, Rector of Southwark Parish, Episcopal Church. p. 18

12 January 1782. John LUCAS and Sarah Andrews. Sur. Thomas Sorsby. p. 9

3 October 1789. John LUCAS and Polly Simmons. Sur. Benjamin E. Brown. Married 10 October by Rev. Samuel Butler, Rector of Southwark Parish, Episcopal Church, who says Mary Simmons. p. 27

23 March 1790. Samuel LUCAS and Polly Watkins, dau. of John Watkins, Sr., who consents and is surety. Married 28 March by Rev. Samuel Butler, Rector of Wouthwark Parish, Episcopal Church, who says Mary Watkins. p. 28

14 May 1789. Thomas LUCAS and Elizabeth Lucas. J(ames?) Kee, guardian of Elizabeth, consents for her. Sur. Christopher Lucas. Wit. N. Barker. p. 26

22 April 1816. William S. LUCAS and Mary Sharp, "of lawful age". Sur. Robert H. Watkins. Wit. Thomas Ellis, Jr. p. 101

7 May 1808. Fed LUMLEY and Patsey Davis. Sur. Samuel Alexander. Married by Rev. Nathaniel Berriman, Methodist. p. 76

26 July 1819. Jesse LUNSFORD and Polly P. Burgess. Sur. Wilie Davis. Wit. Miles Burgess. p. 114

17 March 1792. Thadius LUNSFORD and Nancy Carsley. Sur. Michael Carsley. Married 22 March by Rev. Samuel Butler, Rector of Southwark Parish, Episcopal Church. p. 34

24 July 1820. Thomas LUNSFORD and Matilda V. Bilbro "of full age". Sur. David Booth. p. 117

16 December 1823. George MACKLIN and Patsy Bailey. Sur. Alexander Bailey. Wit. George W. King. Married 18 December by Rev. Isaiah Harris, Elder in the Methodist Church. p. 127

9 January 1813. Archibald MADDERA and Mary Oney, dau. of James Oney, deceased. Sur. Matthew Bruce. Wit. Sarah Howard. Beverly Bruce, guardian of Mary, consents for her. p. 91

22 August 1799. Micajah MADDERA and Lucy Thompson. Sur. Joseph Warren. Wit. Benjamin Barker and Susan Barker. p. 53

28 April 1820. Thomas MADDERA and Rebecca G. Thompson. Sur. Joseph Warren. Married 29 April by Rev. James Warren, Methodist. p. 116

25 February 1812. William MADDERA and Masey Tillott. Sur. William Carseley. Wit. Beverly Booth. p. 88

2 March 1774. Joel MADERA and Lucy Warren. Sur. Thomas Warren. p. 3

2 September 1779. Joel MADERA and Anne Cocke Thompson. Sur.
Thomas Warren. Benjamin Putney, guardian of Anne, consents
for her. p. 7

13 February 1796. James MAHONE and Silvia Medcalf, 21 years
of age. Sur. William Ingram. Wit. William Mahone. Married
18 February by Rev. Nathaniel Berriman, Methodist. p. 43

1 November 1788. Bernard MAJOR and Sarah Sorsby, dau. of
Lucy Sorsby, who consents. Sur. John Southall. Wit. Susanna
Southall. p. 24

23 November 1818. Bernard MAJOR, Jr. and Susan B. Newsum.
Sur. Walter Spratley, Sr. p. 110

28 August 1822. Bernard MAJOR and Mary Westmore. Sur. Francis
Ruffin. Wit. Jesse Lunsford. p. 122

20 December 1771. Harwood MAJOR and Lucy Watson, dau. of
James Watson, who consents. Sur. Robert Pyland. In another
place this marriage is listed as Major Harwood. p. 1

20 December 1787. John MALLICOAT and Mary Gray, dau. of
James Gray, who consents. Sur. Robert McIntosh. p. 22

4 February 1801. John MALLICOTE, Jr. and Elizabeth Webb.
Sur. Samuel Wilson. Married by Rev. Nathaniel Berriman,
Methodist. p. 59

20 October 1783. William MALLORY and Rebecca Eaton, dau. of
William Eaton, deceased. Sur. Robert Hunnicutt. p. 12

5 June 1778. Josiah MANGUM and Sylvia Carrell. Sur. Jeremiah
Pierce. Sylvia born 10 May 1755. Wit. Silvas and Elizabeth
Carrell. p. 6

1 January 1824. Josiah MANGUM and Frances White, dau. of
James White, deceased. Sur. William Delk. p. 128

7 October 1815. Archer MARIAH and Sarah Canady. Sur.
Richard Debrix. Wit. Jonathan Ellis, Matthew Booth and Rebekah
Andrews. p. 98

1 January 1819. Alexander MARKS and Milley Emery. Sur.
Peyton Emery. Wit. Harmon Bishop. p. 112

20 January 1824. Carter MARKS and Elizabeth Hamilin. Married
by Rev. Beverly Booth, Baptist. Ministers' Returns p. 237

29 July 1812. Daniel MARKS and Susannah Sheffield. Sur.
Randolph Johnson. Wit. David Cocke. p. 89

18 June 1785. Henry MARKS and Rebecca Ballard Jarratt, dau.
of John Jarratt, who consents. Sur. John Barlte, Jr. p. 16

26 May 1807. John MARKS and Charlotte Ruffin Bennett, dau.
of William Bennett, who consents. Sur. Richard Mason. Married
28 May by Rev. Nathaniel Berriman, Methodist. p. 74

10 September 1822. John MARKS and Mary G. Emery. Sur. Thomas
Hudgins. p. 122

12 December 1814. Silas MARKS and Matilda Sheffield. Sur.
Samuel Sheffield. Married by Rev. Nathaniel Berriman, Methodist.
p. 96

17 October 1794. John MARSTON and Susanna Dunlop. Sur.
Jacob Faulcon. Wit. Ann Faulcon. Married 19 October by Rev.
Samuel Butler, Rector of Southwark Parish, Episcopal Church.
p. 39

9 July 1792. Alexander MARTIN and Rowena Nimmo. Sur. Andrew
Nimmo. Married 12 July by Rev. Samuel Butler, Rector of
Southwark Parish, Episcopal Church, who says Rowana. p. 34

22 May 1812. William MATHIS and Elizabeth Kee, an orphan,
sister of James Kee, who consents. Neither father nor mother
living. This is consent only. See William Matthews. p. 89

16 January 1796. Daniel MATTHEWS and Rebecca Justiss. Sur.
John Norriss. p. 43

23 May 1812. William MATTHEWS and Elizabeth Kee. Married
by Rev. Nathaniel Berriman, Methodist. See William Mathis.
Ministers' Returns p. 226

23 May 1819. William MATTHEWS and Elizabeth Kee. Sur. Joel
Wall. p. 113

8 October 1821. Dudley MAYNARD and Ann B. Davis, dau. of
Archibald Davis, who consents. Sur. Jonathan Ellis. p. 120

4 November 1793. Edward MAYNARD and Jane Collier. Sur.
Sampson Grantham. Married 5 November by Rev. Samuel Butler,
Rector of Southwark Parish, Episcopal Church. p. 37

8 June 1803. Robert C. MAYNARD and Martha Lucas, dau. of
John Lucas, deceased. Sarah Lucas, mother and guardian of
Martha consents for her. Sur. Herod Summerell. Wit. Sarah
West. Married 9 June by Rev. Nathaniel Berriman, Methodist.
p. 64

5 December 1820. William MAYNARD and Mary H. Hunnicutt. Sur.
William N. Spratley. Married 14 December by Rev. Nathaniel
Berriman, Methodist. p. 118

6 July 1825. Henry O. McENERY and Caroline H. Douglas, dau.
of James Douglas, who consents. Sur. Walter S. Booth. Wit.
Samuel J. Douglas and Peter S. McEnery. Married 7 July by
Rev. Beverly Booth, Baptist. p. 132

26 February 1783. Duncan McGURIMAN and Elizabeth Kerr. Sur.
John Jenkins. p. 11

15 March 1808. James McGURIMAN and Sally Collier "21 years
of age in August 1807." Benjamin Bilbro gives affidavit as
to Sally's age. Sur. Thomas Bilbro. p. 76

23 March 1803. Robert McINTOSH, Jr. and Sally Drew Evans,
dau. of William Evans, deceased. James S. Lane, guardian of
Sally, consents for her. Sur. Robert McIntosh, Sr. p. 63

24 March 1786. Robert McKAY and Mary Ann Catherine Bedolph.
Sur. William Cocke. Married 27 March by Rev. Henry John Burges,
Rector of Southwark Parish, Episcopal Church. p. 18

1 January 1793. John MICHAEL and Polly Walke. Sur. Thomas
Walke. Married 3 January by Rev. Nathaniel Berriman, Deacon
in the Methodist Church. p. 36

28 January 1812. William MILBY and Caroline Brown. Sur.
Jesse P. Warren. Married by Rev. James Hill. p. 87

8 December 1794. Jacob MILLER and Sarah Chapman, dau. of
John Chapman, who consents. Wit. Henley Chapman and David
French. This is consent only. p. 39

13 September 1800. Samuel MILLINGTON and Rebecca E. Clarke.
Sur. William Ingram. Wit. William Slade, Jr. and Anna Pyland.
Married 20 September by Rev. Nathaniel Berriman, Methodist.
p. 57

21 December 1818. James MITCHELL and Polly Davis Mallicote.
Sur. John Mallicote. Married by Rev. Nathaniel Berriman,
Methodist. p. 111

12 January 1801. Blanks MOODY and Patsey Boyce. Sur. William
Boyce. Married by Rev. Nathaniel Berriman, Methodist. p. 59

23 July 1805. Isaac MOODY and Charity Taylor, widow of Charles
Taylor. Sur. Josiah Holleman. Married by William Blunt,
Methodist Minister. p. 69

10 July 1809. Evans MOORE and Martha Hunnicutt. Sur. James
Edwards. Married 11 July by Rev. Nathaniel Berriman, Methodist,
who says Evan. p. 80

14 July 1812. Jesse MOORE and Ann Edwards. Sur. Edwin Edwards.
Married by Rev. Nathaniel Berriman, Methodist. p. 89

11 February 1812. Thomas MOORE and Nancy Cox, dau. of
Benjamin Cox, who consents, and is surety. Married 13 February
by Rev. Nathaniel Berriman, Methodist. p. 87

16 February 1775. Henry MOORING, Jr. and Mary Smith. Sur. John Jarrett. James Smith writes consent that Henry Mooring, Jr. marry Mary Smith, orphan of Henry Smith, deceased. p. 4

27 September 1785. John MORING and Martha Lane. Sur. Thomas Spratley. Wit. Josiah Gray. Married 28 September by Rev. Henry John Burges, Rector of Southwark Parish, Episcopal Church. p. 16

30 September 1797. John MORING and Betsy Smith, dau. of Lucy Smith, who consents. Sur. William Smith. Married 7 October by Rev. Nathaniel Berriman, Methodist. p. 48

6 June 1802. Robert MORING and Polly P. Pyland "of lawful age". Sur. Burwell Barham. Wit. John Scammell and Robert Pyland. Married by Rev. Nathaniel Berryman, Methodist. p. 61

31 March 1812. William MORING and Lucy Cocks. Sur. Benjamin Cocks. Married 2 April by Rev. Nathaniel Berriman, Methodist. p. 88

14 June 1787. John MORRISS and Margaret Calso. Sur. Christopher Moring. p. 21

2 June 1794. John MOYLER and Sally Howard. Sur. Sterling Hill. Married 5 June by Rev. Nathaniel Berriman, Deacon in the Methodist Church. p. 38

27 February 1775. William MITCHELL and Elizabeth (or Eliza) Hodges. Sur. Abraham Mitchell. Wit. Thomas Bland, Jr. p. 4

22 September 1821. Richard MURFEE and Cynthia Shelley. Sur. Jesse P. Warren. Wit. Benjamin Shelley. p. 120

27 February 1787. Joel NEWSOM and Mary Ealy, dau. of John Ealy, who consents. Sur. William Bennett. p. 20

20 November 1821. Robert NEWSOM and Malicy Slade. Sur. Jesse Slade. Wit. Benjamin P. Slade. Married 23 November by Rev. Josiah Harris, Elder in the Methodist Church. p. 120

25 November 1795. Carter NICHOLAS and Ann Hartwell Cocke. Sur. Edward Faulcon. Married 3 December by Rev. Samuel Butler, Rector of Southwark Parish, Episcopal Church. p. 42

28 December 1784. Harris NOCHOLSON and Mary Hargrave. Sur. James Key. p. 14

20 September 1793. Luke NORRIS and Abby Johnson. Sur. Peter Johnson. Married 26 September by Rev. Samuel Butler, Rector of Southwark Parish, Episcopal Church. p. 37

23 January 1798. Luke NORRISS and Martha Johnson. Sur.
Gearmon Ellis. p. 50

11 April 1812. Luke NORRISS and Martha McShavery. Sur.
William Hix. Wit. Miles Burgess. p. 89

24 May 1824. Thomas NORRIS and Elizabeth Dewell, dau. of Wyatt
Dewell, who consents. Sur. Nicholas Dewell. Wit. Howell
Collier. Married by Rev. Beverly Booth, Baptist. p. 128

23 July 1811. Peter OAKWOOD and Roanna H. Dewell "of lawful
age". Sur. William Avriss. Married 7 August by Rev. James
Warren, Methodist. p. 85

7 March 1797. Branch OSBORNE and Ann Harriss. Sur. Colin
Campbell. Married 9 March by Rev. Samuel Butler, Rector of
Southwark Parish, Episcopal Church, who says Nancy. p. 47

24 November 1824. John C. OTEY and Rebecca T. Hunnicutt.
Sur. John Faulcon. p. 130

27 January 1817. Henry OWEN and Nancy R. Justice. Sur.
Edwin Rogers. p. 104

20 April 1789. William OWEN and Ann White, dau. of Henry
White, who consents and is surety. Wit. Edward Faulcon,
Elizabeth Faulcon and Ann Faulcon. p. 26

11 March 1818. Robert H.J. PAGE and Rebekah Marks. Married
by Rev. James Warren, Methodist. Ministers' Returns p. 230

26 September 1805. Richard PADGET and Charity Warren. Sur.
John Ellis. Wit. Michael Smith and Sally E. Smith. Married
28 September by Rev. Nathaniel Berriman, Methodist, who says
Cherry Warren. p. 70

16 July 1816. Talbott PARISH and Mary Lee Harriss. Sur.
Walter Spratley. p. 101

1 December 1789. Benjamin PARKER and Dolly Browne. Sur.
Richard H. Bradford. Married by Rev. Samuel Butler, Rector
of Southwark Parish, Episcopal Church. p. 27

22 September 1791. William PARKER and Catharine McKie.
Sur. Thomas Bartle. Married by Rev. Samuel Butler, Rector of
Southwark Parish, Episcopal Church. Returns dated 26 February
1792. p. 32

13 February 1811. Richard PERSONBY and Silviah Gwaltney
"of age". Sur. Sampson Gwaltney. Wit. Rebecca Gwaltney.
p. 84

19 December 1803. William PARSONS and Mary Tillott, dau. of
John Tillott, who consents. Sur. Robert Parsons. Wit. Thomas
G. Tillott. Married 22 December by Rev. Beverly Booth,
Baptist. See William Persons. p. 65

15 November 1794. William Cocke PARTIN and Elizabeth Clary.
Sur. Wyatt Partin. Married 23 November by Rev. Archer Moody,
Deacon in the Methodist Church. p. 39

25 January 1791. Wyatt PARTIN and Lucy Dewell, dau. of James
Dewell, Jr., who consents. Sur. Drewry Dewell. Wit. Samuel
Andrews. Married 26 January by Rev. Samuel Butler, Rector of
Southwark Parish, Episcopal Church. p. 30

30 March 1795. Jeremiah PEIRCE and Claracy Gilbert. Sur.
Henry Gilbert. See Jeremiah Pierce. p. 40

17 January 1799. Henry PERSON and ------- ---------.
Sur. William Clarke. p. 52

22 February 1819. Richard PERSONBY and Rebecca Riggan.
Sur. Benjamin Riggan. See Richard Ponsonby. p. 112

3 May 1825. Jacob PERSONS and Eliza A. Wilson. Sur. Dawson
Warren. Wit. Mary Clark. p. 132

13 March 1788. Joseph PERSON and Polly Clarke, dau. of
Sampson Clarke, deceased. Martha Clarke, guardian of Polly,
consents for her. Sur. James Carrell. Wit. William Clark
and James Clark. p. 23

22 January 1802. Jesse PERSONS and Frances Gwaltney, dau.
of John Gwaltney, deceased. Sur. Richard Gwaltney. p. 60

19 December 1803. William PERSONS and Mary Tillott, dau. of
John Tillott, who consents. Sur. Robert Parsons. Wit.
Thomas G. Tillott. See William Parsons. p. 65

26 April 1792. Armistead PETER and Elizabeth Blizzard.
Married by Rev. Samuel Butler, Rector of Southwark Parish,
Episcopal Church. See Armstreet Peters. Ministers' Returns
p. 211

27 June 1814. John PETER and Eliza Cocke. Sur. William
Allen. p. 95

9 February 1821. John PETER and Martha Ann Henley. Sur.
John Faulcon. Married 22 February by Rev. Nathaniel Berriman,
Methodist. p. 119

2 July 1782. Robert PETER and Clerimond Holt. Sur. James
Holt. p. 10

24 April 1792. Armstreet PETERS and Elizabeth Blizzard.
Sur. Henry Charity. See Armistead Peter. p. 34

9 January 1796. Jesse PETERS and Sally Debreux. Sur. Armistead
Peters. Married 15 January by Rev. Samuel Butler, Rector of
Southwark Parish, Episcopal Church, who says Debereaux. p. 43

19 September 1786. John PETTWAY and Elizabeth Crafford.
Sur. Thomas Forsyth. p. 19

18 May 1822. Mills E. PHILIPS and Elizabeth Cocks, dau. of
Polly D. Cocks who consents. Sur. James Judkins. p. 122

19 November 1792. Robert PHILLIPS and Mary Barnham. Sur.
Burwell Barnham. p. 35

7 April 1787. William PHILLIPS and Mary Mitchell Thompson,
dau. of John Thompson who consents and is surety. p. 20

16 June 1790. Young PHILLIPS and Sally Williams, dau. of
Mildred Williams who consents. Sur. William Bennett. Wit.
John Williams. Married 17 June by Rev. Samuel Butler, Rector
of Southwark Parish, Episcopal Church. p. 29

15 August 1786. Zachariah PHILLIPS and Rebecca Gwaltney,
dau. of Thomas Gwaltney. Sur. Nathaniel Berriman. p. 19

16 April 1818. William PHRASURE and Susan Slate. Married
by Rev. James Warren, Methodist. See William E. Frazier.
Ministers' Returns p. 230

29 August 1786. Charles PICKETT and Elizabeth Stevens. Sur.
David Charity. p. 19

2 April 1795. Jeremiah PIERCE and Claricy Gilbert. Married
by Rev. Samuel Butler, Rector of Southwark Parish, Episcopal
Church. See Jeremiah Peirce. Ministers' Returns p. 212

26 February 1816. Peter J. PIERCE and Elizabeth Clinch.
Sur. Thomas Ellis, Sr. Married 7 March by Rev. Nathaniel
Berriman, Methodist. p. 100

28 October 1823. Thomas B. PIERCE and Louisa W. Gray. Sur.
Phineas M. Bailey. Wit. Thomas Clinch and Edmund Epps. p. 126

2 February 1815. Thomas PITMAN and Sarah R. Long. Josiah
Holleman, guardian of Sarah, consents for her. Mother Rebecca
Long. Sur. John Drew. Married 18 February by Rev. Nathaniel
Berriman, Methodist. p. 96

27 December 1824. Wilson PITMAN and Martha Taylor. Sur.
Merit Shelly. Married 29 December by Rev. Josiah Bidgood,
Deacon in the Methodist Church. p. 130

23 January 1817. Thomas W. PITT and Miranda Ellis, dau. of
Robert Ellis, who consents. Sur. Jehu N. Barker. Married by
Rev. Nathaniel Berriman, Methodist. p. 104

25 June 1811. Daniel POND and Nancy Hargrove. Sur. Isham
Inman. p. 85

22 February 1819. Richard PONSONBY and Rebekah Riggan. Married
by Rev. Nathaniel Berriman, Methodist. See Richard Personby.
Ministers' Returns p. 231

26 November 1801. Joseph POOL and Susanna Cocke. Sur.
Benjamin Cocke. Married by Rev. Samuel Butler, Rector of
Southwark Parish, Episcopal Church. p. 60

22 November 1808. Allen PORTER and Nancy Rispess. Sur. John
Rispess. Married 24 December by Rev. James Warren, Methodist.
p. 78

12 January 1809. Shadrach PORTER and Levina Bryant. Sur.
James H. Warren. p. 79

25 June 1818. Frederick POWER and Lucy Browne. Sur. William
Randolph. Married by Rev. Nathaniel Berriman, Sr., Methodist.
p. 109

1 January 1821. Daniel PRESSON and Sarah Howard. Sur. Wyatt
Lane. Wit. Beverly Booth. Married 4 January by Rev. Beverly
Booth, Baptist Minister. p. 118

17 December 1804. James PRESSON and Polly Gwaltney, dau.
of William Gwaltney, who consents and is surety. Married by
Rev. John Gwaltney. p. 68

23 June 1823. Nicholas PRESSON and Sally T. Smith, dau. of
Maget Smith (father). Sur. John Maddera. p. 125

20 December 1815. William PRESSON and Delila A. Turner.
Sur. Willis Turner. Wit. Josiah Turner. Married 23 December
by Rev. Nathaniel Berriman, Methodist. p. 99

17 May 1819. Willis PRESSON and Winefred Boman. Sur.
Samuel White. Wit. Hannah Presson and David Davies. p. 113

22 June 1820. Joseph PRETLOW and Elizabeth R. Fitchett.
Sur. William H. Spratley. Married by Rev. Benjamin Devany,
Methodist. p. 117

22 November 1824. Robert PRETLOW and Rowena Fitchett, dau.
of Randolph Fitchett, who consents and is surety. Married
26 November by Rev. Durwell Barrett. p. 130

14 May 1818. Samuel PRETLOW and Dolly Bailey "of full age". Sur. Isaac Bailey. Free negroes. Married 16 May by Rev. Jesse Holleman, Sr. p. 109

25 November 1816. William PRETLOW and Linda ---------, a free woman of color. Sur. John Wilson. Married by Rev. Nathaniel Berriman, Methodist. p. 102

29 April 1799. David PRICE and Susanna McIntosh. Sur. Robert McIntosh. Married 2 May by Rev. Samuel Butler, Rector of Southwark Parish, Episcopal Church. p. 53

16 March 1818. Henry PRICE and Nancy Steward. Sur. William D. Phillips. Henry son of Samuel Price. Married 17 March by Rev. Nathaniel Berriman, Sr., Methodist. p. 108

8 June 1774. Randolph PRICE and Rebecca Hunnicutt. Sur. Robert Hunnicutt. p. 3

15 September 1777. Randolph PRICE and Lucy Hamlen. Sur. William Drew. p. 4

27 December 1796. Samuel PRICE and Elizabeth Phillips. Sur. William Phillips. Married 28 December by Rev. Nathaniel Berriman, Methodist Minister. p. 46

24 October 1824. Samuel PRICE, Sr. and Elizabeth B. Bell. Sur. Joseph Judkins. p. 129

26 February 1825. Samuel PRICE and Sarah T. Davis. Sur. John M. Williams. Wit. James T. Wilson. p. 131

16 December 1797. Thomas PRICE and Nancy Judkins. Sur. Benjamin Bell. Wit. Thomas Judkins. Married 18 December by Rev. Nathaniel Berriman, Methodist. p. 49

27 March 1804. Thomas PRICE and Cecily Cofer. Married by Rev. Nathaniel Berriman, Methodist. See Thomas Tann. Ministers' Returns p. 220

26 May 1814. Thomas PRICE and Priscilla Jones. Sur. Williamson Talley. Married by Rev. Nathaniel Berriman, Methodist. p. 95

24 January 1789. Tobias PRICE and Sarah Brown. Sur. William Hart, Jr. p. 25

9 November 1818. Jeremiah PROCTOR and Ann B. Holt. Sur. William Hunnicutt. Married 10 November by Rev. Nathaniel Berriman, Methodist. p. 110

3 January 1825. John J. PULLY and Mourning H. Hargrave. Sur. John Holt. Married 18 January by Rev. Nicholas Presson. p. 131

7 February 1780. David PUTNEY and Elizabeth Goodman Collins. Sur. Benjamin Putney. Elizabeth, dau. of William Collins, who writes consent. p. 8

23 December 1802. Henry PUTNEY and Elizabeth Putney. Married by Rev. James Warren, Methodist Minister. Ministers' Returns p. 218

13 August 1799. Benjamin PYLAND and Betsy Lane. Sur. John Moring. Married 15 August by Rev. Nathaniel Berriman, Methodist. p. 53

8 February 1788. James PYLAND and Sally White. Sur. John Pierce. Wit. Jeremiah Pierce and George Mallicote. James Pyland of Isle of Wight County. p. 22

21 December 1812. James PYLAND and Marinda Holt. Sur. Joseph Berriman. Wit. Thomas Rowell. Married 24 December by Rev. Nathaniel Berriman, Methodist. p. 90

25 November 1816. James PYLAND and Sally S. Jones. Sur. Thomas J. Pyland. Wit. John Wilson. Married 26 November by Rev. Nathaniel Berriman, Methodist. p. 102

3 April 1789. Obediah PYLAND and Sally Harriss. Sur. John Slade. p. 25

22 March 1796. Obediah PYLAND and Lucy Clarke. Sur. John Pyland. Married by Rev. Nathaniel Berriman, Methodist Minister. p. 44

24 September 1787. Thomas PYLAND and Lucy Judkins. Sur. Albridgton Seward. p. 21

29 December 1818. Thomas J. PYLAND and Patsey Adams. Sur. John P. Hopkins. Wit. Joseph Barham. Married by Rev. Nathaniel Berriman, Methodist. p. 111

17 March 1825. Benjamin A. RAE and Mary C. Velvin. Sur. Boling Ellis. p. 132

7 January 1778. James RAE and Hannah Andrews. Sur. John Ellis. p. 5

27 December 1788. William RAE and Mary Andrews. Sur. William Andrews. p. 25

19 December 1799. William RAE and Emelia Collier. Sur. Blanks Moody. p. 54

25 June 1821. William RAMEY and Martha Rogers, dau. of Micajah Rogers, who consents. Sur. Richard Carter. Married 3 July by Rev. James Warren, Methodist. p. 120

19 March 1806. Peter RANDOLPH and Sally L. Cocke. Sur. William Randolph, Jr. p. 71

28 October 1795. Simon RANDOLPH and Frances Patterson. Sur. Luke Taylor. p. 41

23 December 1772. William RANDOLPH and Mary Kennon. Sur. Allen Cocke. William Ruffin, Jr., guardian of William Randolph, consents. p. 1

13 February 1800. William RANDOLPH, Jr. and Martha Seward "of age". Sur. Patrick H. Adams. Wit. Sally Norsworth and James Smith. Married 20 February by Rev. Samuel Butler, Rector of Southwark Parish, Episcopal Church. p. 55

20 April 1809. William RANDOLPH and Hannah Browne. Sur. Charles H. Graves. p. 80

25 March 1807. William REAVES, Jr. and Rebecca Seward, dau. of Albridgeton Seward. Sur. Carter Seward. Wit. Joel Willsinson. See William Rives, Jr. p. 73

18 March 1799. Thomas T. RELFE and Martha H. Watkins. Sur. John Watkins. p. 52

28 July 1787. Benjamin RHOADS and Sarah Fitchett. Sur. William Adams. Wit. Josiah Gray. p. 21

2 September 1802. John RICHARDSON and Elizabeth Shuffield. Sur. Thomas M. Johnston. p. 61

20 January 1802. Jordan RICHARDSON and Lucy Wren, dau. of John Wren, who consents and is surety. Married 27 January by Rev. Drewry Lane. p. 60

7 February 1818. Benjamin RIGGAN and Nancy Lane. Sur. David Long. p. 107

26 May 1823. Benjamin RIGGAN and Matilda Edwards. Sur. Nelson Edwards. Wit. Richard Murfee. p. 125

14 November 1810. Francis RIGGAN and Rebecca P. Armstrong. Sur. Richard Drewry, Jr. Wit. Richard D. Riggan. p. 83

25 January 1799. Ira RIGGAN and Catharine Warren. Sur. William Riggan. Married by Rev. James Warren, Methodist Minister. p. 52

2 January 1800. John RIGGAN and Sucky Savidge, widow of Nathaniel Savidge. Sur. William Cryer. Married by Rev. Nathaniel Berriman, Methodist. p. 55

19 December 1791. William RIGGAN and Ann Warren. Sur. James Drewry. Wit. John Riggan and Benjamin Riggan. p. 33

30 January 1796. William RIGGAN and Sarah Holleway. Sur. William Bennett. Married 2 February by Rev. Nathaniel Berriman, Methodist, who says Holloway. p. 43

17 September 1790. John RIGGIN and Elizabeth Warren, dau. of Ann Warren, Executrix, who consents. Sur. Benjamin Biggers. Wit. John Reed and John Warren. John Riggin son of William Riggin. p. 29

13 January 1816. William RIPLEY and Sarah Harper Jones. Sur. James Jones. Married 18 January by Rev. Nathaniel Berriman, Methodist. p. 100

7 December 1795. Christopher RISPESS and Nancy Smith, dau. of Mary Smith who is also Nancy's guardian and consents for her. Sur. William Clinch, Jr. Married 10 December by Rev. Nathaniel Berriman, Methodist Minister, who says Rispes. p. 42

5 April 1800. John RISPESS and Mary A. Dews. Sur. James Clarke. Wit. John Smith. Married 12 April by Rev. Nathaniel Berriman, Methodist. p. 56

14 June 1804. John RISPESS and Elizabeth Edwards "21 years of age". Sur. Thomas D. Edwards. Married by Rev. Nathaniel Berriman, Methodist. p. 67

22 September 1811. Burwell RIVES and Martha Stephens. Married by Rev. James Warren, Methodist. Ministers' Returns p. 223

25 March 1807. William RIVES, Jr. and Rebecca Seward, dau. of Albridgeton Seward. Sur. Carter Seward. Wit. Joel Wilkinson. Married 26 March by Rev. Nathaniel Berriman, Methodist. See William Reaves, Jr. p 73

9 February 1810. Daniel RIX and Lucy Bailey, dau. of Isaac Bailey, who is surety. Daniel a free negro liberated by Robert Rix of Southampton County. Lucy a free negro. p. 82

17 May 1802. Joseph ROBERTS and Elizabeth Charity, dau. of David Charity, who consents and is surety. Married by Rev. James Warren, Methodist Minister. p. 61

23 March 1786. Samuel ROBERTS and -------- Harrison. Married by Rev. Henry John Burgess, Rector of Southwark Parish, Episcopal Church. Ministers' Returns p. 208

8 August 1821. Allen ROGERS and Polly Bartle. Sur. Caufield Hunnicutt. Wit. Thomas King. Married 9 August by Rev. James Warren, Methodist. p. 120

10 June 1823. Allen ROGERS and Sally Riggan "of lawful age". Sur. Benjamin Riggan. Wit. William Slade and Ira Riggan. p. 125

28 February 1795. Benjamin ROGERS and Elizabeth Wren. Sur. John Wren. p. 40

24 November 1817. Edwin ROGERS and Lucy Collier "21 years of age". Sur. John Collier. Wit. George C. Collier. p. 106

22 January 1791. Richard ROGERS and Cherry Wren. Sur. Benjamin Rogers. p. 30

9 November 1804. Stephen ROGERS and Mildred Ellis, "of lawful age", dau. of Cherry Watkins. Sur. David Sebrell. Wit. John Watkins. Married 22 November by Rev. Drewry Lane. (Cherry Ellis m. John Watkins, Jr. 9 Oct. 1798.). p. 68

21 May 1787. William ROGERS and Martha Harris. Sur. Charles Holdsworth. p. 21

28 February 1789. Enoch ROLFE and Elizabeth Watkins, dau. of John Watkins, who consents and is surety. p. 25

30 July 1821. Peyton R. ROSE and Susanna S. Crittenden. Sur. John M. St. George. p. 120

27 March 1810. James ROWELL and Betsy Gray. Sur. Henry Gray. Married by Rev. Nathaniel Berriman, Methodist. p. 83

14 November 1825. James ROWELL and Polly Mabra Carrell. Sur. James R. Seward. Married 17 November by Rev. John Engles, Baptist. p. 133

24 February 1823. Richard ROWELL and Rebecca Holt, dau. of Francis Holt, who consents and is surety. Married 6 March by Rev. Josiah Bidgood, Deacon in the Methodist Church. p. 124

24 December 1793. Samuel ROWELL and Sally Berriman. Sur. Robert Pyland. Married by Rev. Nathaniel Berriman, Deacon in the Methodist Church. p. 37

22 December 1796. Robert ROWELL and Lucy Berriman, dau. of Nathaniel Berriman, Sr. Sur. Joseph Berriman. Wit. Nathaniel Berriman, Jr. Married 24 December by Rev. Nathaniel Berriman, Methodist Minister. p. 46

27 December 1803.   Thomas ROWELL and Sally Davis "21 years of age", dau. of Winfred Davis, (mother).   Sur. James Edwards. Married by Rev. John Gwaltney who says Sarah. p. 65

8 February 1809.   Thomas ROWELL and Ann Berriman, dau. of Nathaniel Berriman, Sr.   Sur. Nathaniel Berriman, Jr.   Married 9 February by Rev. Nathaniel Berriman, Methodist.   p. 79

23 May 1823.   James RUFF and Betsy Alias Betsy Blizard, "of lawful age".   Sur. William Blizard.   Wit. John Slade, Jr. and Lizar Anderson.   p. 125

3 January 1775.   Francis RUFFIN and Hannah Cocke, dau. of John Cocke, who consents.   Sur. Allen Cocke.   Wit. John Hawkins, Jr.   Wit. to consent Mary and Thomas Cocke.   p. 3

11 November 1782.   Francis RUFFIN and Susanna Harris, dau. of William Harris, who consents.   Sur. John Hartwell Cocke. p. 10

4 September 1817.   Francis RUFFIN and Mariah Wilson.   Sur. William H.T. Browne.   Married by Rev. Nathaniel Berriman, Sr., Methodist.   p. 105

29 August 1799.   George RUFFIN and Rebecca Cocke.   Sur. William Ruffin.   Married 19 September by Rev. Samuel Butler, Rector of Southwark Parish, Episcopal Church.   p. 54

20 January 1810.   James RUFFIN and Betsy Bird.   Sur. Wright Walden.   Wit. Archibald Davis.   p. 82

25 November 1795.   William RUFFIN and Ann Edwards, dau. of William Edwards, who consents and is surety.   p. 42

13 February 1824.   William E.B. RUFFIN and Martha R. Edwards. Sur. Richard H. Edwards.   p. 128

19 November 1772.   Samuel RUSSELL and Priscilla Lanier.   Sur. Sylvanus Gregory.   p. 1

7 February 1825.   Acrill SAVEDGE and Ursley Warren.   Sur. Nicholas Warren.   Wit. Thomas S. Lane.   Rebecca Bell, mother and guardian of Ursley, consents for her.   p. 131

18 December 1815.   Allen SAVEDGE and Lucy Slade, dau. of John Slade, Sr.   Sur. Burwell Savedge.   Wit. William Slade, Jr. and Clemmy Slade.   Married 21 December by Rev. Nathaniel Berriman, Methodist.   p. 99

26 February 1821.   Benjamin SAVEDGE and Elizabeth Owen.   Sur. John C. Judkins.   Wit. Daniel Presson.   p. 119

18 October 1820. Burwell SAVEDGE and Louisa Tynes, dau. of
Louisa Tynes, who consents. Sur. John Tynes. Married 19
October by Rev. Nathaniel Berriman, Methodist. p. 117

10 November 1818. Champion SAVEDGE and Hannah Rogers. Sur.
William Spratley. Married 12 November by Rev. Nathaniel ·
Berriman, Methodist. p. 110

28 September 1818. Joel SAVEDGE and Polly Carrell. Sur.
Nathaniel Spratley. Wit. Jesse J. Carrell. Married 29
September by Rev. Nathaniel Berriman, Methodist. p. 109

21 December 1819. Wiley T. SAVEDGE and Martha Cockes. Sur.
John Carrell. Wit. John N. Carrell. Married 22 December by
Rev. Nathaniel Berriman, Methodist. p. 115

16 January 1793. David SAVIDGE and Naome Porter. Sur.
Nathaniel Savidge. Married 23 January by Rev. Nathaniel
Berriman, Deacon in the Methodist Church. p. 36

27 November 1804. Doiley SAVIDGE and Susanna Smith. Sur.
Joel Savidge. Married by Rev. Nathaniel Berriman, Methodist.
p. 68

6 December 1782. Hartwell SAVIDGE and Selah Brown, dau. of
James Brown, who consents and is surety. p. 11

20 February 1796. Hezekiah SAVIDGE and Sally Batts "of age".
Sur. Henry Warren. Wit. Sally Warren. Married 25 February
by Rev. Nathaniel Berriman, Methodist. p. 44

13 March 1782. Joel SAVIDGE and Rebecca Ward. Sur. Hartwell
Savidge. p. 10

8 June 1789. Josiah SAVIDGE and Susanna Cheatham, dau. of
Becky Cheatham, who consents. Sur. Thomas Bland, Jr. Wit.
Stephen Cheatham and Scarbrough Jones. Married 14 June by
Rev. Samuel Butler, Rector of Southwark Parish, Episcopal
Church. p. 27

11 December 1798. Moses SAVIDGE and Martha James. Sur.
Moland James. Married 15 December by Rev. Nathaniel Berriman,
Methodist. p. 52

26 October 1787. Samuel SAVIDGE and Lucy James. Sur.
Nathaniel Savidge. p. 21

12 December 1814. John SCAMMELL and Lucy Adams. Sur. John
Mallicote. Wit. Joseph Barham and James Adams. Married 15
December by Rev. Nathaniel Berriman, Methodist. p. 96

17 October 1778. Richard SCAMMELL or Schamell and Cilviah
Maddara. Sur. John Moreland. p. 6

21 June 1796. William SCAMMELL and Martha McIntosh. Sur.
Robert McIntosh. Married 23 June by Rev. Samuel Butler,
Rector of Southwark Parish, Episcopal Church. p. 44

11 October 1797. James SCARBROUGH and Susanna Bishop. Sur.
Stephen Shuffield. p. 49

20 April 1810. Grayham SCOTT and Patsy Andrews, dau. of Beckey
Andrews. Sur. David Charity. Married 22 April by Rev. James
Hill. p. 83

24 December 1819. Joseph SCOTT and Mary Holdsworth. Sur.
Dempsey Bowers. Wit. Rebecca Holdsworth. Married 25 December
by Rev. Josiah Bidgood, Deacon in the Methodist Church. p. 116

28 December 1792. William SCOTT and Edy Charity, dau. of
Elizabeth Charity, who consents. Sur. Major Debrix. Married
30 December by Rev. Nathaniel Berriman, Deacon in the Methodist
Church. p. 35

25 January 1821. Samuel SEARS and Mary Ann Wilson. Married
by Rev. James Warren, Methodist. Ministers' Returns p. 235

23 March 1815. Capt. David SEBRELL and Anner H. Watkins.
Sur. Thomas Bailey. Wit. John Watkins. p. 97

26 March 1817. George SEMPLE and Elizabeth A. Holt. Sur.
Armistead Russell. Married 27 March by Rev. Nathaniel Berriman,
Methodist. p. 104

28 May 1814. Albridgton SEWARD and Elizabeth Pyland, widow.
Sur. William Cocks, Jr. Wit. Samuel Sorsby. Albridgton
Seward, a widower. Married 29 May by Rev. Nathaniel Berriman,
Methodist. p. 95

8 October 1800. Carey SEWARD and Polly I'Anson Thorp. Sur.
Albridgeton Seward. Married 11 October by Rev. Nathaniel
Berriman, Methodist. p. 57

30 May 1798. Caufield SEWARD and Hannah Ruffin. Sur. Carter
Nicholas. Married 31 May by Rev. Samuel Butler, Rector of
Southwark Parish, Episcopal Church. p. 51

24 July 1820. Edward SEWARD and Polly Rowell. Sur. Jesse J.
Carrell. Wit. James B. Seward. See Edwin Seward. p. 117

29 April 1814. Edwin SEWARD and Sally Cocks, dau. of William
Cocks, Sr., who consents. Sur. William Cocks, Jr. Wit.
Wyatt Cocks. Married by Rev. Nathaniel Berriman, Methodist.
p. 94

27 July 1820. Edwin SEWARD and Polly Rowell. Married by
Rev. Nathaniel Berriman, Methodist. See Edward Seward.
Ministers' Returns p. 232

29 June 1772. William Caufield SEWARD and Ann (illegible).
Sur. William Drew. p. 1

10 November 1777. William Caufield SEWARD and Mary Ann Faulcon.
Sur. Nicholas Faulcon, Jr. p. 5

23 November 1815. William SEWARD and Nancy Savedge "of
lawful age". Sur. Thomas Maddera. Married 25 November by
Rev. Nathaniel Berriman, Methodist. p. 98

13 February 1800. Levingston SHANNON and Elicia Ann St. George,
"of age". James Simpson gives affidavit as to Elicia's age.
Sur. Roland Holt. Married 16 February by Rev. Samuel Butler,
Rector of Southwark Parish, Episcopal Church, who says <u>Alicia</u>
and <u>Livingston</u>. p. 55

24 December 1792. Burwell SHARP and Sarah White. Sur. James
White. Married 25 December by Rev. Nathaniel Berriman,
Deacon in the Methodist Church. p. 35

23 August 1824. Nicholas SHARP and Maria Rogers, dau. of
Benjamin Rogers, who consents. Sur. William S. Lucas. Wit.
John L. Rogers, Robert Holsworth and Thomas Sharp. Married
26 August by Rev. Beverly Booth, Baptist. p. 129

15 June 1794. Richard SHELL and Lucy Barker. Sur. John
Barker. Wit. Rebecca Barker. Married 23 June by Rev. Samuel
Butler, Rector of Southwark Parish, Episcopal Church. p. 38

11 January 1794. Benjamin SHELLEY and Elizabeth Gwaltney,
dau. of Thomas Gwaltney, who consents. Sur. Zachariah Phillips.
Wit. Ann Gwaltney. p. 38

10 December 1796. Benjamin SHELLY and Martha Bell. Sur.
Benjamin Bell. Married 17 December by Rev. Nathaniel Berriman,
Methodist. p. 45

27 June 1799. John SHELLY and Rebecca Barlow. Sur. Shadrach
Goodrich. Married by Rev. Nathaniel Berriman, Methodist. p. 53

23 May 1801. John Gibbons SHARP and Elizabeth S. White.
Sur. Thomas Ellis, Jr. Married by Rev. Nathaniel Berriman,
Methodist. p. 59

30 January 1816. Archibald SHEFFIELD and Susanna R. Clark.
Sur. Jesse P. Warren. p. 100

21 December 1814. Pleasant SHEFFIELD and Elizabeth Bishop,
dau. of James Bishop, who consents. Sur. Carter Marks. Wit.
Peyton Emery. p. 96

28 December 1792. James SHUFFIELD and Elizabeth Bagley.
Sur. Andrew Kelsey. Married by Rev. Samuel Butler, Rector of
Southwark Parish, Episcopal Church. p. 35

16 January 1808. James SHUFFIELD and Rebecca Hite. Sur.
Nicholas Hite. Wit. Robert Booth. p. 76

19 September 1785. Peter SHUFFIELD and Sally Emery. Sur.
Wyatt Emery. Wit. Josiah Gray. Married by Rev. Henry John
Burges, Rector of Southwark Parish, Episcopal Church. p. 16

23 October 1812. Henry SIKES and Sally Holleman. Sur. Travis
Phillips. p. 90

25 April 1786. William SIMMONS and Rebekah Lucas. Sur.
James Kee. p. 19

12 June 1824. Thomas SIMPSON and Sally Wallace. Sur. Thomas
Clinch. p. 128

29 May 1801. Arthur SINCLAIR and Eliza Cocke. Sur. James
S. Lane. Married by Rev. Samuel Butler, Rector of Southwark
Parish, Episcopal Church. Return dated 26 November. p. 59

23 July 1791. John SINCLAIR and Mary I'Anson. Sur. Charles
Hanson. Married by Rev. Samuel Butler, Rector of Southwark
Parish, Episcopal Church. p. 32

31 January 1791. Benjamin SLADE and Mary Cogging. Sur.
James Clark. Married 3 February by Rev. Samuel Butler,
Rector of Southwark Parish, Episcopal Church, who says
Coggin. p. 31

12 March 1800. Clemmy SLADE and Polly Tynes. Sur. William
Slade. Wit. James T. Emery and Mary Judkin. Married 15
March by Rev. Nathaniel Berriman, Methodist. p. 56

15 December 1800. Jesse SLADE and Mary James, dau. of Jeremeah
and Silviah James who consent. Sur. Moreland James. Wit.
Thomas Cocke, Jr. and Burwell Savidge. William Slade, father
of Jesse, consents for him. Married by Rev. Nathaniel Berriman,
Methodist. p. 58

17 February 1786. John SLADE and Elizabeth Holloway, dau.
of Lazarus Holloway, who consents and is surety. Married
21 February by Rev. Henry John Burgess, Rector of Southwark
Parish, Episcopal Church. p. 18

10 November 1788. John SLADE, Jr. and Molly Holloway, dau.
of Lazarus Holloway, who consents. Sur. William Slade, Jr.
p. 24

14 November 1789. John SLADE and Sarah Judkins. Sur. Obadiah
Pyland. Wit. John Judkins, Jr. and James Judkins. Married
17 November by Rev. Samuel Butler, Rector of Southwark Parish,
Episcopal Church. p. 27

10 September 1817. John SLADE, Jr. and Margaret Holt. Sur.
Thomas Slade. Wit. Lusey Shufield. p. 106

7 February 1809. Thomas SLADE and Betsy Slade. William
Slade, Jr. consents for Betsy; no relationship stated. Sur.
Burwell Savidge. Wit. John Seward and Benjamin Slade. Married
9 February by Rev. Nathaniel Berriman, Methodist, who says
Elizabeth. p. 79

2 January 1787. William SLADE and Sally Holloway, dau. of
Lazarus Holloway, who consents. Sur. John Slade. p. 20

17 April 1793. William SLADE and Martha Holt. Sur. Thomas
Holt. Married 30 April by Rev. Nathaniel Berriman, Deacon in
the Methodist Church. p. 36

25 August 1795. Hubert SLEDGE and Martha Wall, "of age",
dau. of Thomas Wall, deceased. Sur. James Wall. Wit. Will
Boyce and Joseph Holt. p. 41

11 November 1796. Lemuel Clay SLEDGE and Jane Fugler. Sur.
Henry Dewell. Married 29 November by Rev. Archer Moody,
Deacon in the Methodist Church. p. 45

12 December 1771. John SMALLY and Penelope Hunnicutt. Sur.
James Gray. p. 1

23 February 1780. Francis SMITH and Martha Grantham. Sur.
Sampson Grantham. p. 8

19 December 1788. James SMITH and Mary Drew Judkins, dau.
of Charles Judkins, who consents. Sur. Joseph Thorp. p. 25

22 July 1794. James SMITH and Susanna Warren "of age". Sur.
Samuel Carrell. Wit. Thomas Warren. Married 14 August by
Rev. Nathaniel Berriman, Deacon in the Methodist Church. p. 38

18 February 1800. James SMITH and Sally Norsworthy, "of age".
Sur. Patrick H. Adams. Wit. Martha Seward and William Randolph,
Jr. Married 20 February by Rev. Samuel Butler, Rector of
Southwark Parish, Episcopal Church. p. 55

18 June 1822. James SMITH and Ann Lane, dau. of John Lane,
who consents. Sur. James Lane. p. 122

25 December 1798. John SMITH and Mary Moody. Sur. Blanks
Moody. Married by Rev. Drewry Lane. p. 52

14 September 1815. Joshua SMITH and Mrs. Elizabeth Parker.
Sur. Jesse Sikes. Married 15 September by Rev. James Warren,
Methodist. p. 98

28 March 1799. Maget SMITH and Mary L. Holt. Sur. Christopher Rispes. p. 52

11 October 1779. Michael SMITH and Rebecca Respess (or Rispess). Sur. Benjamin Barham. p. 7

16 December 1816. Nathaniel SMITH and Elizabeth N. Seward "of lawful age", dau. of Rebekar Seward, who consents. Sur. Edwin Seward. Wit. Polly M. Seward and John Seward. Married 18 December by Rev. Nathaniel Berriman, Methodist. p. 102

24 October 1817. Ned SMITH and Amy Brown, free people of color. Sur. Moses Pretlow. Wit. Moses Johnson. p. 106

3 January 1825. Philip SMITH and Martha Ann Price. Sur. Henry Southall. p. 131

18 January 1819. Samuel SMITH and Mary W. Wall. Sur. Drury Carrell. Wit. William Wall. p. 112

28 January 1774. William SMITH and Anne Mooring, dau. of Henry Mooring, who consents. Sur. John Judkins. Wit. William Nelson and Rebecca Thompson. p. 2

26 December 1825. Wyatt SMITH and Parthenia Vallentine "of lawful age". Sur. Benjamin B. Bailey. Wit. Mark Booth and Rebekah D. Booth. p. 133

23 March 1786. George SOLOMON and Lucy Emery. Sur. Peter Johnson, Jr. Wit. Thomas Emery and Thomas Bishop. Married 24 March by Rev. Henry John Burges, Rector of Southwark Parish, Episcopal Church. p. 18

22 May 1792. Stephen SORSBY and Rebecca Cocks. Sur. John Watkins, Sr. p. 34

1 January 1822. Henry SOUTHALL and Rebecca R. Price, dau. of David Price, who consents. Sur. Philip Smith. p. 121

18 December 1784. John SOUTHALL and Susanna Sorsby. Sur. John Lucas, Jr. John Southall of James City County. p. 14

23 September 1793. John SPRATLEY and Ann Pettway. Sur. John Pettway. Married 26 September by Rev. Samuel Butler, Rector of Southwark Parish, Episcopal Church. p. 37

1 November 1799. John SPRATLEY and Sally Hart. Peter Hamlin, guardian of Sally, consents for her. Sur. Benjamin Cocke. Wit. James L. Lane and Edwin D. Hart. Married 5 November by Rev. Samuel Butler, Rector of Southwark Parish, Episcopal Church. p. 54

22 January 1811. John SPRATLEY and Martha Gray Hart. Sur.
Walter Spratley. James S. Lane, guardian of Martha, consents
for her. Married 24 January by Rev. Nathaniel Berriman,
Methodist. p. 84

1 October 1822. John N. SPRATLEY and Sarah H. Carsley. Sur.
John Faulcon. p. 122

26 October 1818. Nathaniel SPRATLEY and Lucy Cocks. Sur.
John Cocks. Married 12 November by Rev. Nathaniel Berriman,
Methodist, who says Cox. p. 110

27 January 1812. Peter Thomas SPRATLEY and Margaret S. Wilson,
dau. of Samuel Wilson whose consent is dated 27 January 1813.
Sur. Walter Spratley, Jr. Married 28 January 1813 by Rev.
Nathaniel Berriman, Methodist. p. 87

27 January 1813. Peter T. SPRATLEY and Margaret S. Wilson,
dau. of Samuel Wilson, who consents. This is consent only.
p. 91

23 October 1816. Peter T. SPRATLEY and Mary Wheadon Gilbert.
John Randolph, guardian of Mary, consents for her. Sur.
James Wheadon. Wit. Joel Savedge and Lucy Brown. Married
by Rev. Nathaniel Berriman, Methodist. p. 102

6 May 1783. Thomas SPRATLEY and Ann Holdsworth. Sur. Michael
Smith. p. 12

24 May 1808. Walter SPRATLEY and Elizabeth Shackleton, dau.
of Rd. (Richard?) Shackleton who consents. Sur. George Judkins.
Married 26 May by Rev. Nathaniel Berriman, Methodist, who says
Shackleford. p. 77

2 August 1821. Walter SPRATLEY, Sr. and Sarah W. Newsum.
Married by Rev. Benjamin Holt Rice, Presbyterian Minister.
Ministers' Returns p. 235

8 December 1823. Walter SPRATLEY, Sr. and Rebecca B. Hinton.
Sur. John N. Spratley. Wit. Nancy Spratley. p. 127

5 April 1773. William SPRATLEY and Ann Faulcon, dau. of
Nicholas Faulcon, Sr., who consents. Sur. Nicholas Faulcon,
Jr. p. 2

-- December 1791. William SPRATLEY and Mary White. Sur.
William Clinch, Jr. p. 34

19 November 1796. William SPRATLEY and Margaret Warren. Sur.
Samuel Warren. Married 21 November by Rev. Nathaniel Berriman,
Methodist. p. 45

22 July 1806. William SPRATLEY and Dolly Hamlin. Sur. John Faulcon, Jr. Wit. John Spratley. Married 24 July by Rev. Nathaniel Berriman, Methodist. p. 71

15 June 1825. William H. SPRATLEY and Sally B. Pierce. Sur. P.T. Spratley. p. 132

11 December 1811. Abraham STALLINGS and Winnefred Persons, dau. of Polly Persons, who consents. Sur. Benjamin C. Bell. Wit. Henry Person. Married by Rev. John Gwaltney. p. 87

13 February 1821. Joseph STEPHENSON and Elizabeth Sledge. Sur. Richard Ellis. Married 20 February by Rev. Williamson Hoskins Pittman. p. 119

29 January 1768. Joseph STEVENSON and Martha Newsum, dau. of Joseph Newsum, who consents. Sur. John Newsum. p. 1

28 December 1790. William STEWARD and Celia Bell. Sur. Hartwell Hart. Wit. Will Salter. See William Stewart. p. 30

7 February 1800. Stewart, a free negro of Sussex County and Rachel, a free negro liberated by Ano^I Bailey. Sur. Jesse alias Jesse Bailey, a free negro. p. 55

27 November 1787. Jesse STEWART and Sylvia Clary. Sur. Samuel Hargrave. p. 21

15 September 1817. Jesse STEWART and Elizabeth Thompson. Sur. Robert H. Watkins. Wit. Miles Burgess and Robert H. Cocks. p. 106

11 October 1808. Samuel STEWART and Lucy Scott. Sur. David Charity. Married 13 October by Rev. James Warren, Methodist, who says Lucy Charity. p. 78

14 December 1802. Stephen STEWART and Nancy Sheffield "21 years of age", dau. of James Sheffield. Sur. Thomas M. Johnston. p. 62

8 June 1781. William STEWART and Faithy Hughes. Sur. William Grantham. p. 9

27 January 1791. William STEWART and Celia Bell. Married by Rev. Samuel Butler, Rector of Southwark Parish, Episcopal Church. See William Steward. Ministers' Returns. p. 209

9 December 1782. John STILES and Mary Sebrell. Sur. Burwell Sharp. p. 11

22 July 1788. John STILES and Jane Cooper "of age". Sur. William Ellis. Wit. Stephen Sorsby. p. 23

22 December 1812. John STILES and Rebecca Cooper. David
Sebrell, guardian of Rebecca, consents for her. Sur. Miles
Burgess. p. 90

17 April 1809. Leroy STILES and Anna Hickman. Sur. James
Bishop. Wit. Thomas G. Tillott and Daniel O. Matthews. Leroy
son of John Stiles. p. 80

2 March 1813. Drury STITH and Elizabeth S. Ellis. Sur.
William Edwards. Married 4 March by Rev. Nathaniel Berriman,
Methodist. p. 91

12 April 1806. Henry SUFFIELD and Ann Marks "upward of 21
years of age:. Sur. William Hix. Wit. Randolph Johnson. p. 71

22 December 1788. William TALIAFERRO and Elizabeth Hartwell
Cocke. Sur. Richard Cocke, Jr. p. 25

27 March 1804. Thomas TANN, alias Thomas Price and Selah
Cofer "21 years of age". Sur. Thomas Cofer. Wit. Thomas
Shelley and George Pettit. Married by Rev. Nathaniel Berriman,
Methodist, who says Cecily. p. 66

24 December 1793. Aaron TAYLOR and Milley Scott. Sur. Armistead
Peters. Married 29 December by Rev. Nathaniel Berriman,
Deacon in the Methodist Church. p. 37

23 December 1799. Aaron TAYLOR and Elsey Charity, dau. of
David Charity. p. 54

30 September 1795. Capt. Charles B. TAYLOR and Lucy Jones
"of age". Sur. James Wilson. Wit. Lucy Person. Married 1
October by Rev. Nathaniel Berriman, Methodist. p. 41

8 February 1819. Charles TAYLOR and Jamima Gwaltney. Sur.
Jacob Person. Wit. Martha Gwaltney. p. 112

15 January 1803. Jordan TAYLOR and Winny Crocker "22 years of
age and upwards". Sur. Josiah Davis. Married by Rev. John
Gwaltney who says Winefred. p. 63

14 December 1789. Robert TAYLOR and Elizabeth Ward. Sur.
Edward Burt. Married 17 December by Rev. Samuel Butler, Rector
of Southwark Parish, Episcopal Church. p. 28

15 December 1814. Robert TAYLOR and Elizabeth Watkins Cryer
"21 years of age", dau. of William Cryer. Sur. James D.
Edwards. Wit. Rebekah B. Clarke. Married 22 December by
Rev. Nathaniel Berriman, Methodist. p. 96

25 March 1788. Thomas TAYLOR and Rebecca Gray. Sur. Zachariah
Phillips. p. 23

5 February 1789. David THOMAS and Rebecca Anthony, dau. of
William Anthony, who consents. Sur. John Anthony. p. 25

17 December 1818. James THOMAS and Mary Dewell "of lawful age".
Sur. Stephen Andrews. Married 24 December by Rev. James Warren,
Methodist. p. 111

11 January 1795. Jesse THOMAS and Elizabeth Presson. Sur.
John Presson. p. 40

25 January 1814. Joel THOMAS and Polly Presson. Sur. John
M. Williams. Married by Rev. John Gwaltney. p. 94

12 December 1786. Matthew THOMAS and Ann Gwaltney, dau. of
John Gwaltney, who consents and is surety. p. 20

5 June 1776. Micajah THOMAS and Elizabeth Crafford. Sur.
Carter Crafford. p. 4

10 September 1791. Philip THOMAS and Lucy Holleman. Sur.
John Holleman. p. 32

24 May 1803. Richard THOMAS and Lucy Hunnicutt, dau. of
Hartwell Hunnicutt, who consents and is surety. Married 31
May by Rev. Nathaniel Berriman, Methodist. p. 64

1 September 1780. Samuel THOMAS and Katharine Carrell, dau.
of Eliza Carrell, who consents. Sur. George Mallicot. p. 8

25 November 1807. Henry THOMPSON and Martha Warren, dau. of
Rebecca Warren, who consents. Sur. Richard Mason. Married
26 November by Rev. Nathaniel Berriman, Methodist. p. 75

19 July 1820. John N. THOMPSON and Elizabeth S. Crittenden.
Thomas P. Gwaltney, guardian of John N. Thompson. Sur. Thomas
L. Barham. Wit. Baylor Dudley. Married 20 July by Rev.
Nathaniel Berriman, Methodist. p. 117

3 April 1821. John E. THOMPSON and Elizabeth Bell "above
21 years of age", dau. of Stephen Bell, deceased. Sur. William
Ingram. Wit. Nicholas Judkins. Married by Rev. Nathaniel
Berriman, Methodist. p. 119

11 September 1804. Nathaniel THOMPSON and Nancy Dewell, dau.
of Henry Dewell, who consents. Sur. James Clinch. Wit.
Elizabeth Dewell. p. 67

11 December 1800. Nicholas Hart THOMPSON and Polly Gwaltney.
James P. Bell, guardian of Polly, consents for her. Sur.
William Ingram. Wit. Samuel Bell and Willis Thompson. Married
15 December by Rev. Nathaniel Berriman, Methodist. p. 57

18 September 1790. Samuel THOMPSON and Edy Deberix. Sur.
Howell Debreux. p. 29

28 September 1791. Sim THOMPSON and Sally Thompson. Sur.
Richard Scammell. Married 29 September by Rev. Samuel Butler,
Rector of Southwark Parish, Episcopal Church. p. 33

21 November 1812. Thomas M. THOMPSON and Mrs. Nancy Jones
"of full age". Sur. John M. Williams. p. 90

8 January 1796. William Evans THOMPSON and Hannah Barner Holt.
Sur. William Holt. Married 9 January by Rev. Nathaniel
Berriman, Methodist Minister. p. 43

26 December 1797. William THOMPSON and Martha Macshafery.
Sur. William Johnson. p. 50

11 May 1805. William Evans THOMPSON and Susan Bell, dau. of
Benjamin Bell, who consents and is surety. Married by Rev.
Nathaniel Berriman, Methodist. p. 69

12 March 1808. Willis THOMPSON and Catharine Holt. Sur.
Joseph Berriman. Married 15 March by Rev. Nathaniel Berriman,
Methodist. p. 76

18 June 1798. John TILLOTT and Lucy Grantham. Sur. Michael
Caseley or Carsley. p. 51

28 February 1804. John TILLOTT and Elizabeth Andrews "of
lawful age". Sur. Miles Burgess. Wit. John Justiss. p. 66

18 February 1804. Thomas G. TILLOTT and Masey Oney. Sur.
Hartwell Carseley. Wit. Beverly Booth. Married by Rev.
Beverly Booth, Baptist. p. 66

10 December 1821. Merit M. R. TODD and Martha Ridley Persons,
dau. of Mary Persons, who consents. Sur. Bartholomew Lightfoot.
p. 121

22 December 1777. Benjamin TURNER and Rebekah Grantham, dau.
of Thomas Grantham, who consents and is surety. p. 5

19 November 1787. Jesse TURNER and Lucy Brown. Sur. Thomas
Cofer. p. 21

2 April 1811. Josiah TURNER and Polly Judkins. Sur. Thomas
Judkins. Wit. Willis Thomas. James Logan, guardian of Josiah,
consents for him. Married 4 April by Rev. Nathaniel Berriman,
Methodist. p. 85

11 December 1789. Matthew TURNER and Nancy Brown. Sur.
William Cornwell. Matthew Turner of Isle of Wight County.
p. 27

4 October 1791. Thomas TURNER and Olive Login. Sur. John Wright. Wit. Ann Faulcon. p. 33

19 February 1788. Vines TURNER and Ann Adams. Sur. Nathaniel Adams. p. 23

24 November 1817. William TURNER and Averilla Goodrich. Sur. Hardy Harris. Wit. Zachariah Harris. p. 106

23 August 1808. Willis TURNER and Elizabeth Briggs. Sur. John Briggs. Married 25 August by Rev. Nathaniel Berriman, Methodist. p. 77

26 August 1823. Willis TURNER and Ann G. Glover. Sur. Thomas Maddera. p. 126

3 January 1821. James TYNES and Elizabeth Banks "of legal age". Sur. Willis Banks. This bond reads: James, alias Tynes and Elizabeth, alias Banks. p. 118

24 September 1806. John TYNES and Rebecca Pyland "over 21 years of age". Sur. Clemmy Slade. Wit. Mary Slade. Married 2 October by Rev. Nathaniel Berriman, Methodist. p. 72

28 May 1804. Nicholas Scott VALENTINE and Keziah Charity "24 years of age", dau. of Judith Charity. Sur. Wright Walden. Wit. Nathan Jones, Jr., Howell Collier and Polly Howell. p. 67

21 June 1814. Randolph VALENTINE and Elizabeth Peters "upwards of 21 years of age". Negroes. Nicholas Scott, a mulatto, makes affidavit as to Elizabeth's age and is surety. Married 23 June by Rev. James Warren, Methodist. p. 95

23 December 1800. John VELVIN and Permelia Cooper. Sur. Miles Burgess. p. 58

19 December 1774. James VICK and Sally Nicolson. Sur. William Nelson. See James Wicks. p. 3

29 July 1790. Drewry WALDEN and Hannah Scott, dau. of Nicholas Scott, who consents. Sur. Armistead Peters. Wit. James Bailey. Married 1 August by Rev. Samuel Butler, Rector of Southwark Parish, Episcopal Church. p. 29

9 August 1809. John WALDEN and Eady Canada. Sur. James B. Dowden. Married 10 August by Rev. James Hill. p. 80

6 April 1793. Sampson WALDEN and Scillar Porter, 21 years of age, dau. of Edward Porter. Sur. Howell Debrix. Wit. William Andrews and Nathaniel Andrews. Married 7 April by Rev. Nathaniel Berriman, Deacon in the Methodist Church. p. 36

5 December 1784. Stephen WALDEN and Ann Bartel of <u>Sussex County</u>. Sur. David Debrix. p. 14

2 February 1778. William WALDEN and Priscilla Banks, dau. of John Banks, who consents and is surety. p. 6

30 March 1804. Wright WALDEN and Sally Byrd, dau. of Joseph Byrd, who consents. Sur. James Williams. Wit. Joseph Ellis. p. 66

27 February 1787. Thomas WALKE and Ann Holt. Sur. William Hart. p. 20

29 May 1774. Robert WALKER and Susanna Harrison. Sur. Nathaniel Harrison, Jr. p. 3

30 March 1790. Joel WALL and Rebecca Gibbons. Sur. Benjamin Cocke. Married 1 April by Rev. Samuel Butler, Rector of Southwark Parish, Episcopal Church. p. 28

-- November 1811. Joel WALL and Nancy W. Gwaltney, dau. of Sarah Gwaltney, who consents. Sur. Cordy Wombwell. Wit. James P. Bell. Married by Rev. John Gwaltney. p. 86

14 March 1814. Patrick H. WALL and Polly Edmunds Warren, dau. of Drewry P. Warren who consents. Sur. Joel Wall. p. 94

24 June 1780. John Owen WALLACE and Elizabeth Bennett. Sur. Thomas Warren. p. 8

24 March 1812. John WALLACE and Ann Briggs. Sur. Albridgton Seward. Married 7 April by Nathaniel Berriman, Methodist. p. 88

14 April 1789. Wilson WALLIS and Catharine Cocke. Sur. Richard Cocke. p. 26

24 November 1785. William WARBURTON and Nancy Morris. Married by Rev. Henry John Burgess, Rector of Southwark Parish, Episcopal Church. Ministers' Returns. p. 207

4 May 1808. William WARD and Delphia Gwaltney. Sur. Sampson Gwaltney. Wit. Syllviah Gwaltney. William Ward of <u>Isle of Wight County</u>. p. 76

3 February 1802. Frederick N. WARREN and Sally Edwards. Sur. Benjamin Bell, Jr. Wit. William Mitchell. Married 5 February by Rev. Nathaniel Berriman, Methodist. p. 60

23 April 1805. Frederick WARREN and Mary Williams. Sur. William Bennett, Jr. Married 25 April by Rev. Nathaniel Berriman, Methodist. p. 69

26 November 1792. Henry WARREN and Sally Phillips. Sur. John Davis, Jr. Married 29 November by Rev. Nathaniel Berriman, Deacon in the Methodist Church. p. 35

9 October 1789. James WARREN and Katy Andrews, dau. of John Andrews, who consents. Sur. Benjamin Warren. Wit. Fanny Andrews and Lucy Andrews. p. 27

15 January 1798. James H. WARREN and Becca Lane. Sur. Frederick Lane. Married 1 February by Rev. Nathaniel Berriman, Methodist. p. 50

21 December 1812. Jesse WARREN and Martha Thompson. Sur. Joseph Davis. Wit. Willis Thompson. Married 14 January 1813 by Rev. Nathaniel Berriman, Methodist. p. 90

25 January 1814. JesseP. WARREN and Sally Bell "21 years of age". Sur. William Warren. Wit. Benjamin Bell. Married by Rev. Nathaniel Berriman, Methodist. p. 94

21 December 1790. John WARREN and Jane Davis. Sur. John Davis. Married 23 December by Rev. Samuel Butler, Rector of Southwark Parish, Episcopal Church. p. 30

15 October 1797. John D. WARREN and Cherry Lane. Jesse Moore and Rebecca Moore, guardians of Cherry, consent for her. Sur. Joel Lane. Wit. James H. Warren and Samuel Bell. Married by Rev. Nathaniel Berriman, Methodist. p. 49

25 December 1820. John A. WARREN and Lucy Thompson. Sur. Henry Andrews. Married 28 December by Rev. James Warren, Methodist. p. 118

7 February 1814. Joseph WARREN and Eliza Savedge "21 years of age". Robert Mooring makes affidavit as to Eliza's age. Sur. Phil. Smith. Married 10 February by Rev. Nathaniel Berriman, Methodist. p. 94

22 December 1812. Judkins WARREN and Sally Simmons. Sur. Drewry P. Warren. Married 26 December by Rev. Nathaniel Berriman, Methodist. p. 90

10 February 1804. Lemuel WARREN and Patsy Lane, dau. of Sally Lane. Sur. Samuel Warren. Married 16 February by Rev. Nathaniel Berriman, Methodist. p. 66

14 April 1825. Randolph WARREN and Jane Ellis "upward of 21 years of age". Sur. James R. Thompson. p. 132

21 December 1796. Samuel WARREN and Charity Cary "of age". Sur. Charles Emery. Wit. Dorothy Emery. Married 24 December by Rev. Nathaniel Berriman, Methodist. p. 46

27 May 1800. Samuel WARREN and Cherry Bell. Sur. Benjamin Bell. Married 31 May by Rev. William Browne. p. 56

11 February 1806. Samuel WARREN, Jr. and Patsy Warren, dau.
of Jesse Warren, deceased. Sur. Benjamin Bell, Sr. Married
13 February by Rev. Nathaniel Berriman, Methodist. p. 71

6 March 1795. Thomas WARREN and Elizabeth Gardner. Sur.
John Davis. Married 7 March by Rev. Nathaniel Berriman,
Methodist Minister. p. 40

26 January 1799. Thomas WARREN and Mary R. Moring. Sur.
Benjamin Cocks. p. 52

10 May 1821. Thomas WARREN and Mary Ann Berriman, dau. of
Nathaniel Berryman, Jr. Sur. William H. Finch. Thomas son of
John Warren, deceased. Charles H. Graves, guardian of Thomas
Warren. Married 15 May by Rev. Nathaniel Berriman, Sr.,
Methodist. p. 120

26 March 1790. William WARREN and Elizabeth Davis. Sur.
William Clinch, Jr. Married 3 April by Rev. Samuel Butler,
Rector of Southwark Parish, Episcopal Church. p. 28

12 February 1824. William WARREN and Nancy L. Lane. Married
by Rev. Beverly Booth, Baptist. Ministers' Returns p. 237

22 February 1819. Willis D. WARREN and Polly Edwards. Sur.
Allen Warren. p. 112

5 April 1819. James WARTHEN and Nancy Thompson. Sur.
William Evans Thompson. Married 6 April by Rev. Nathaniel
Berriman, Methodist. p. 113

25 October 1774. Nicholas WASHINGTON and Sarah Holdsworth.
Sur. Rebecca R. Holdsworth. p. 3

9 October 1798. John WATKINS, Jr. and Cherry Ellis. Sur.
John Watkins, Sr. p. 51

28 October 1798. Joseph WATKINS and Sally Porter, dau. of
Edward Porter, who consents and is surety. Wit. Elizabeth
Porter. p. 23

23 March 1818. Robert H. WATKINS and Elizabeth S. Sharp.
Sur. David Sebrell. Wit. Robert Holdsworth. p. 108

7 September 1785. James WATSON and Peggy Wilson, dau. of
Josiah Wilson, Gentleman, who consents. Sur. Harwood Calcote.
Married 8 September by Rev. Henry John Burges, Rector of
Southwark Parish, Episcopal Church. p. 16

24 December 1811. John L. WELLIN and Sally M. Mallicote.
Married by Rev. Nathaniel Berriman, Methodist. See John
Lewellin. Ministers' Returns p. 224

14 January 1786. Robert WELLINGS and Sally Wooten. Married by Rev. Henry John Burgess, Rector of Southwark Parish, Episcopal Church. This bond is in Southampton as Wellons and Wooton. (Knorr: Southampton p. 112) Ministers' Returns p. 207

15 September 1812. John WESTMORE and Mary Lunsford, dau. of Thaddeus Lunsford, who consents. Sur. William Carseley. Wit. Nancy Lunsford. Married 15 October by Rev. James Hill. p. 89

23 October 1816. James W. WHEADON and Mary White. Sur. Peter T. Spratley. Married by Rev. John Gwaltney. p. 102

12 July 1813. James WHEATON and Sarah Hunnicutt. Sur. Robert Hunnicutt. Married 15 July by Rev. Nathaniel Berriman, Methodist. p. 92

28 December 1813. Edwin WHITE and Jane Holleman. Sur. Josiah Holleman. Married by Rev. John Gwaltney. p. 93

18 December 1797. James WHITE and Martha Evans Judkins. Sur. Charles Judkins. Married 24 December by Rev. Nathaniel Berriman, Methodist Minister. p. 49

28 December 1813. James WHITE, Jr. and Ann Delk. Sur. Josiah Holleman. Married by Rev. John Gwaltney who says Nancy. p. 93

15 March 1824. Robert WHITE and Ann Scammell Taylor "of lawful age". Sur. Thomas Clinch. Wit. Henry L. Guthrie and Martha Andrews. p. 128

5 June 1786. Samuel WHITE and Mary Clary, dau. of Mary Clary, who consents. Sur. Charles Holdsworth. Wit. Thomas Burgess and James Judkins. Married 7 June by Rev. Henry John Burges, Rector of Southwark Parish, Episcopal Church. p. 19

20 October 1818. Samuel WHITE and Mrs. Lucy Davis. Sur. William E. Bailey. p. 110

28 February 1782. Thomas WHITE and Averilla Smith, widow of Allen Smith. Sur. Anthony Degge. p. 10

28 November 1795. Walter WHITE and Rebecca Edwards "of age". James and Mary Holloway make affidavit as to age of Rebecca; no relationship stated. Sur. Wyatt Sharp. Wit. James White. Married 3 December by Rev. Drewry Lane. p. 42

1 April 1795. Warren WHITE and Lucy Presson. Sur. John White. Married 2 April by Rev. Samuel Butler, Rector of Southwark Parish, Episcopal Church, who says Preston. p. 40

13 March 1823. William WHITE and Lucinda Lane. Married by Rev. Williamson Hoskins Pittman. Ministers' Returns p. 234

24 May 1818. Willis WHITE and Olive Bailey "21 years of age", dau. of Isaac Bailey, who is surety. Free negroes. Married 28 May by Rev. Jesse Holleman, Sr. p. 109

28 October 1823. Holleman WHITEMORE and Frances Warren "of lawful age", dau. of James Warren, who consents. Sur. Alexander Bailey. Wit. John A. Warren. Married by Rev. Isaiah Harris, Elder in the Methodist Church. p. 126

21 October 1825. John WHITMORE and Elizabeth M. Warren "of lawful age". Sur. James Warthen. Wit. Lucinda Carter. p. 133

7 January 1809. Francis WICKER and Eliza Hopkins. Sur. Stephen A. Hopkins. Married 8 January by Rev. Nathaniel Berriman, Methodist. p. 79

19 December 1774. James WICKS and Sally Nicolson. Sur. William Nelson. See James Vick. p. 3

28 May 1811. Abram WILLIAMS and Rebecca Moore, dau. of Jesse Moore, who consents. Sur. John M. Williams. Married 30 May by Rev. Nathaniel Berriman, Methodist. p. 85

8 April 1788. Frederick WILLIAMS and Mary Hutchings. Sur. Richard Edwards. p. 23

12 April 1823. Hugh WILLIAMS and Susanna Davis, both of lawful age. Sur. Matthew Booth. p. 125

6 November 1813. James WILLIAMS and Pamelia Debrix, 35 years of age. Sur. Nicholas Scott. Wit. Howell Collier. Married 11 November by Rev. James Warren, Methodist. p. 92

25 October 1819. James WILLIAMS, Jr. and Kizziah Blizzard. Sur. James Williams, Sr. Married 28 October by Rev. Beverly Booth, Baptist. p. 115

26 March 1782. Jeremiah WILLIAMS and Martha Mitchell. Sur. William Mitchell. p. 10

23 January 1815. John M. WILLIAMS and Mary Thomas. Sur. Matthew Thomas. Wit. Peter T. Spratley. Married 2 February by Rev. Nathaniel Berriman, Methodist. p. 96

31 October 1824. John WILLIAMS and Nancy Holloway. Sur. Silas Holloway. Wit. Baalam Wright and Mary Ann Holloway. p. 130

23 December 1815. Nathaniel H. WILLIAMS and Martha Marks. John J. Marks, guardian of Martha, consents for her. Sur. George Anderson. Married by Rev. Nathaniel Berriman, Methodist. p. 99

12 February 1791. Thomas WILLIAMS and Mary Williams "of age".
N. Harrison, with whom she lives, makes affidavit as to Mary's
age. Sur. William Bennett. Wit. Nathaniel Stewart and William
Collins. Married 14 February by Rev. Samuel Butler, Rector
of Southwark Parish, Episcopal Church. p. 31

10 September 1807. Thomas WILLIAMS and Patsy Hart. Sur.
John Marks. p. 75

22 May 1815. William WILLIAMS and Elizabeth Thomas. Sur.
Matthew Thomas. Married 8 June by Rev. Nathaniel Berriman,
Methodist. p. 97

7 April 1798. David Flowers WILLIAMSON and Parthenia Lucas.
Sarah Lucas, guardian of Parthenia, consents for her. Sur.
Bartley Andrews. Wit. Joseph Williamson. Married by Rev.
Samuel Butler, Rector of Southwark Parish, Episcopal Church.
p. 50

9 January 1817. Joseph WILLIAMSON and Mary Maddera. Sur.
Hezekiah Savedge. Wit. Wilie T. Savedge. Married by Rev.
Nathaniel Berriman, Methodist. p. 103

8 January 1796. Bela WILLIFORD and Elizabeth Parker. Sur.
John Tillott. p. 43

16 February 1797. James WILLIFORD and Susan D. Cheatham.
Sur. James Rae. p. 47

28 December 1772. Augustine WILLIS and Ann Heath, widow of
John Heath. Sur. Allen Cocke. Wit. William Nelson. p. 1

13 March 1788. Lewis WILLIS and Elizabeth Cocke, dau. of
Henry Cocke, deceased. Sur. Lemuel Cocke. p. 23

4 December 1809. Colin C. WILLS and Elizabeth Cary. Sur.
Josiah Savidge. Wit. Rebecca B. Clarke and Charity Paget.
Married 15 December by Rev. Nathaniel Berriman, Methodist,
who says Collin. p. 81

23 January 1785. Nathaniel WILLS and Mildred Coman. Sur.
Archibald Wills. Married 28 February by Rev. Henry John
Burges, Rector of Southwark Parish, Episcopal Church. p. 14

9 July 1784. William WILLS and ------ ------. Sur. Archer
Holt. Wit. Thomas Bland, Jr. p. 13

25 November 1777. James WILSON and Mary I'Anson. Sur. William
Short. p. 5

31 May 1786. James WILSON and Faithy Banks, dau. of John
Banks, who consents. Sur. Joseph Roberts. p. 19

22 September 1795. Samuel WILSON and Betsy Boyce. Sur.
William Boyce. Married 24 September by Rev. Nathaniel Berriman,
Methodist Minister. p. 41

20 December 1796. William WILSON and Sally Delk. Sur. Sampson
Wilson. Married 24 December by Rev. Nathaniel Berriman,
Methodist. p. 46

29 July 1797. William WILSON and Sarah Blizard. Sur. Peter
Blizard. p. 48

3 December 1785. Reuben WINDHAM and Jane Clements. Married
by Rev. Henry John Burgess, Rector of Southwark Parish,
Episcopal Church. Ministers' Returns p. 207

26 September 1825. Thomas WISER and Susan B. Major. Sur.
John Burt (or Burke). See Thomas Wizer. p. 133

-29 September 1825. Thomas WIZER and Susan B. Major. Married
by Rev. Isaiah Harris, Elder in the Methodist Church. See
Thomas Wiser. Ministers' Returns p. 236

22 December 1796. Benjamin WOMBLE and Martha Balmer Price.
William Holt, guardian of Martha, consents for her. Sur.
William Adams. Married 26 December by Rev. Nathaniel Berriman,
Methodist, who says Barner. p. 46

6 January 1812. Cordy WOMBWELL and Lucy Wall, dau. of Charity
Wall, who consents. Sur. Joel Wall. Married by Rev. John
Gwaltney. p. 87

25 February 1800. Thomas WOMBWELL and Sally Gray. Sur. Henry
Gray. Married 27 February by Rev. Nathaniel Berriman, Methodist.
p. 55

30 October 1788. Jonathan WOOD and Mary Handy. Sur. Jeremiah
Banks. p. 24

24 December 1805. Joseph WOOD and Ann B. Moring. Sur.
William Moring. Married 2 January 1806 by Rev. Nathaniel
Berriman, Methodist. p. 70

27 April 1818. James H. WOODLEY and Mary Wilson. Sur. Andrew
Woodley. Married 30 April by Rev. John Blunt, Deacon in the
Methodist Church. p. 108

4 October 1785. Thomas WOOTON and Mary Tomlinson. Married
by Rev. Henry John Burgess, Rector of Southwark Parish,
Episcopal Church. This bond is in Sussex dated 1 Oct. 1785.
Mary, an orphan, her guardian William Tomlinson consents.
Sur. Miles Birdsong. Wit. Joseph Birdsong and John Tomlinson.
(Knorr: Sussex p. 88) Ministers' Returns p. 207

15 February 1796. Josiah WRENN and Frances Brown "of age".
Sur. Josiah Wilson. Wit. Martha Wilson. Married 18 February
by Rev. Nathaniel Berriman, Methodist. p. 44

22 June 1807. Richard WRENN and Sally Hargrave. Sur. John
Clark. Richard Wrenn of Southampton County. Married 30 June
by Rev. Drewry Lane. p. 74

11 July 1796. Thomas WRENN and Nancy Boyce. Sur. William
Boyce. p. 44

25 January 1819. Thomas WRENN and Polly Hart. Sur. Thomas
Atkins. Married 27 January by Rev. Burwell Barrett. p. 112

30 November 1818. Augustine WRIGHT and Keziah Judkins "above
21 years of age". Sur. Nicholas Judkins. Wit. John Williams
and Josiah Turner. Married by Rev. Nathaniel Berriman, Methodist.
p. 110

12 April 1786. Isham WRIGHT and Nancy Carter, dau. of Mourning
Carter (mother), who consents. Sur. William Carter. p. 18

17 March 1812. James WRIGHT and Nancy Slade, "both of lawful
age". Sur. Clemmy Slade. Wit. William Slade and Betty Slade.
Married 19 March by Rev. Nathaniel Berriman, Methodist. p. 88

26 December 1797. John WRIGHT and Marenda Smith. Sur. James
Davis. Married 27 December by Rev. Nathaniel Berriman,
Methodist Minister, who says Maranda. p. 49

26 February 1811. Littleton WYNN and Sarah Mann. Sur. John
Watkins. John Peter, guardian of Sarah, consents for her. p. 85

24 January 1775. Richard YARBROUGH and Sarah Watkins. Sur.
John Watkins. p. 3

18 September 1800. Francis YOUNG and Elizabeth Nelson, dau.
of Anne Nelson, who consents. Sur. John Goodrich. p. 57

20 May 1783. James YOUNG and Ann Nelson. Sur. William
Nelson. p. 12

Booke,
   Edith, 6

Boardman,
   Elizabeth, 3

Boazman,
   Lucy, 23

Boman,
   Winefred, 66

Booth-Bouth,
   Ann Davis, 28
   Sarah, 47

Bowser,
   Keziah, 44

Boyce,
   Betsy, 91
   Lucy, 52
   Nancy, 92
   Patsey, 61

Bradby,
   Ann Hunt, 1
   Catherine Allen, 42

Bride,
   Mary M., 9

Bridges,
   Susanna, 15

Briggs,
   Aggy, 55
   Ann, 85
   Elizabeth, 84
   Rebecca, 40

Bristow,
   Mary, 19

Brockwell,
   Elizabeth, 9

Brown,
   Amy, 78
   Betsy, 55
   Caroline, 61
   Elizabeth, 37
   Frances, 91
   Jane, 43
   Lucy, 66, 83
   Mary, 23
   Nancy, 83
   Patty, 6
   Rebecca, 4
   Sarah, 44, 67
   Selah, 73

Browne,
   Dolly, 63
   Elizabeth, 37
   Hannah, 69
   Patsy, 37
   Rebecca, 4
   Sally Edwards, 11

Bruce,
   Lucy, 4

Bryant,
   Levina, 66
   Rebecca, 49
   Sally B., 28

Buchanan,
   Susanna, 29

Bunkley,
   Keziah, 57

Burgess,
   Martha, 22
   Polly P., 58
   Rebecca, 16

Burn,
   Sally, 1

Burt,
   Ann J., 49
   Ann Judkins, 49
   Elizabeth, 22

Byrd,
   Betsy, 72
   Sally, 85

C

Calso,
   Margaret, 62

Campbell,
   Elizabeth, 1, 51
   Mary Lee, 40

Canada,
   Edy, 84

Canady,
   Sarah, 59

Carrell,
   Ann, 32
   Katharine, 82
   Nancy, 5
   Polly, 73
   Polly Mabra, 71
   Rebecca, 16
   Sally, 35
   Susanna, 18, 46
   Sylvia, 59

Carseley-Carsley,
   Anna, 5
   Eliza, 9
   Margaret, 12
   Nancy, 23, 58
   Polly C., 55
   Rebecca B., 43
   Sarah H., 79

Carter,
   Ann, 57
   Charity, 57
   Mary, 28
   Nancy, 38, 92
   Susan, 57

Cary,
   Anne, 23
   Charity, 86
   Elizabeth, 90

Caseley,
   Martha, 31

Champeon,
   Mary, 28

Champion,
   Mary, 56

Chapman,
   Sarah, 61

Chappell,
   Mary, 6

Charity,
   Anne, 26
   Charlotte, 17
   Clary, 18

Charity, Cont'd.
   Edy, 74
   Elizabeth, 70
   Elsey, 81
   Keziah, 84
   Lucretia, 18
   Mary, 10
   Mason, 18
   Nancy, 57
   Rebecca, 2
   Sarah, 35

Chatham,
   Elizabeth, 10

Cheatham,
   Polly, 22
   Sally, 5
   Susan D., 90
   Susanna, 73

Clark,
   Lucy, 37
   Mary W., 1
   Nancy, 32
   Sally, 39
   Susanna R., 75

Clarke,
   Elizabeth, 41
   Lucy, 68
   Polly, 64
   Rebecca E., 61

Clary,
   Elizabeth, 64
   Mary, 88
   Sylvia, 80

Clements,
   Jane, 91

Clinch,
   Anna, 12
   Elizabeth, 65
   Mary, 23, 47
   Rebecca, 22
   Sarah, 32

Cocke,
   Ann Hartwell, 62
   Ann Hunt, 12
   Anne, 13
   Catharine, 85
   Eliza, 64, 76
   Elizabeth, 12, 90
   Elizabeth Hartwell, 8
   Hannah, 72
   Jane, 11
   Lucy, 29, 79
   Martha, 45
   Martha Ann, 43
   Martha B., 43
   Martha R., 14
   Mary H., 29
   Mary Kennon, 33
   Mary Stark, 41
   Polly Stark, 41
   Rebecca, 72
   Sally, 34
   Sally L., 69
   Susanna, 1, 66

Cockes,
   Lucy, 42
   Martha, 73
   Martha R., 21

Cocks,
   Elizabeth, 53, 65
   Lucy, 62
   Nancy, 40
   Rebecca, 78

Holt, Cont'd.
  Clerimond, 64
  Dolly, 36
  Elizabeth A., 74
  Elizabeth E., 45
  Elizabeth W., 16
  Hannah Barner, 83
  Keziah, 8
  Margaret, 77
  Marinda, 68
  Martha, 77
  Mary, 23
  Mary L., 78
  Rebecca, 38, 71
  Susanna H., 8

Hopkins,
  Eliza, 89

Howard,
  Sally, 62
  Sarah, 66

Howell,
  Polly, 17

Hughes,
  Faithy, 80

Hunnicutt,
  Ann Binns, 46
  Lucy, 82
  Martha, 61
  Mary, 47
  Mary H., 60
  Penelope, 77
  Rebecca, 67
  Rebecca T., 63
  Sarah, 88

Hutchings,
  Mary, 89

I

I'Anson,
  Mary, 76, 90
  Nancy, 29

Ingram,
  Eliza, 17
  Jemima, 7
  Polly, 53

Inman,
  Elizabeth, 44
  Sally D., 13

Irby,
  Mary, 31

J

James,
  Lucy, 73
  Martha, 73
  Mary, 76
  Nancy, J., 32
  Rebekah, 48
  Susanna, 33

Jarrett,
  Rebecca, 59

Jemm,
  Eliza, 19
  Mary Ann, 39

Jenkins,
  Elizabeth, 9

Jimm,
  Elizabeth, 13

Johnson,
  Abby, 62
  Amy, 13
  Betsy, 50
  Frances, 32
  Giley, 54
  Gilly, 54
  Martha, 23, 63
  Mildred, 14, 43
  Rebekah, 11

Jones,
  Elizabeth, 18
  Lucy, 81
  Martha, 50
  Nancy, 83
  Peggy, 20
  Priscilla, 67
  Sally S., 68
  Sarah, 31
  Sarah Harper, 70

Jordan,
  Elizabeth, 27

Judkins,
  Ann, 51
  Ann F., 10
  Ann Lamb, 14
  Charity, 45
  Cherry, 45
  Elizabeth, 14, 48
  Elizabeth W., 9
  Hannah, 1
  Keziah, 92
  Lucy, 57, 68
  Martha Evans, 88
  Martha Wilkins, 8
  Mary, 19
  Mary Ann, 52
  Mary Drew, 77
  Nancy, 67
  Polly, 46, 83
  Rebecca, 48, 54
  Sally, 17
  Sally Hart, 26
  Sarah, 76

Justice,
  Nancy R., 63
  Rebecca, 60
  Sarah, 16

Justiss,
  Peggy, 37
  Rhoda, 27
  Sarah, 16

K

Kee,
  Elizabeth, (2) 60
  Jane, 16
  Mary Ann, 41
  Rebecca, 21
  Sally, 30,
  Susan, 27

Kennon,
  Mary, 69

Kerr,
  Elizabeth, 61

Key,
  Elizabeth Lascelles, 4

King,
  Ann, 18
  Lucy B., 3
  Polly B., 4

L

Lancaster,
  Mary, 5

Lane,
  Ann, 44, 77
  Becca, 86
  Betsy, 6, 68
  Cherry, 86
  Eliza M., 44
  Elizabeth W., 40
  Louisa N., 8
  Lucinda, 88
  Lucy, 52
  Martha, 62
  Mary, 52, 53
  Nancy, 46, 51, 69
  Nancy L., 87
  Patsy, 86
  Peggy, 25
  Rebecca, 5
  Sally, 8, (2) 25
  Susanna, 13

Lanier,
  Dorothy, 32
  Priscilla, 72

Little,
  Charlotte, 50
  Conney, 50
  Elizabeth (2) 54
  Mary, 51
  Sarah, 17

Login,
  Olive, 84

Long,
  Charlotte, 30
  Nancy, 56
  Sarah R., 65

Love,
  Frances, 40

Lucas,
  Ann Rebecca, 43
  Betty, 23
  Elizabeth, 58
  Jane, 41
  Margaret, 52
  Martha, 60
  Mary, 8, 57
  Mary S., 20
  Parthenia, 90
  Rebekah, 76

Lunsford,
  Mary, 88

Mc

McIntosh,
  Ann, 10
  Martha, 74
  Sally, 42
  Susanna, 67

McKie,
  Catharine, 63

McShavery,
  Martha, 63

M

Mackie,
  Martha Wright, 48
  Mary, 48

97

Macshafery,
  Martha, 83

Maddera,
  Cilviah, 73
  Diana, 24
  Lucretia, 38
  Mary, 90
  Priscilla, 17

Major,
  Susan B., (2) 91

Mallecote,
  Elizabeth, 45
  Louisa W., 37
  Peggy, 56
  Polly Davis, 61
  Sally McIntosh, 56
  Sally M., 87

Mann,
  Sarah, 92

Marks,
  Ann, 34, 81
  Elizabeth, 9
  Frances, 10
  Martha, 89
  Rebecca, 3
  Rebecca B., 3
  Rebekah, 63
  Tempeah, 50

Marriott,
  Sarah, 24
  Susan A., 51

Maynard,
  Cassandra, 31
  Virginia H.L., 19

Mead,
  Nancy, 29

Meads,
  Mary, 10

Medcalf,
  Silvia, 59

Meed,
  Nancy, 29

Mitchell,
  Martha, 89

Monroe,
  Susanna, 18

Moody,
  Hannah, 47
  Mary, 77
  Rebecca, 32

Moore,
  Elizabeth, 25
  Margaret, 28, 52
  Rebecca, 89

Moring,
  Ann, 20
  Anne, 78
  Ann B., 91
  Elizabeth, 55
  Elizabeth E., 21
  Mary, 28
  Mary R., 87
  Rebecca, 49
  Sarah, 6, 22
  Susanna, 39, 54

Morris,
  Nancy, 85

N

Nelson,
  Ann, 92
  Elizabeth, 92

Newell,
  Martha Ann, 5
  Patty, 3

Newsom,
  Anner H., 15
  Martha Ruffin, 20

Newsum,
  Eliza C., 29
  Martha, 80
  Martha Ruffin, 20
  Sarah W., 79
  Susan B., 59

Norsworthy,
  Sally, 77

Nicolson,
  Sally, 84, 89

Nimmo,
  Harriot, 4
  Helena Reid, 56
  Rowena, 60

O

Oney,
  Mary, 58
  Masey, 83

Owen,
  Elizabeth, 72

P

Padget-Padgett,
  Charity, 26

Page,
  Rebecca, 19

Parker,
  Elizabeth, 77, 90
  Sarah T., 43

Parr,
  Eliza, 41

Parsons,
  Sarah, 35

Partin,
  Dorcas, 28

Partridge,
  Bramble, 6

Patterson,
  Frances, 69

Perry,
  Elizabeth, 49

Persons,
  Martha Ridley, 83
  Winefred, 80

Peter,
  Claramond, 23
  Elizabeth, 20

Peters,
  Anna, 26
  Eliza, 1
  Elizabeth, 84

Pettett,
  Rebecca, 16

Pettway,
  Ann, 78
  Sarah, 46

Phillips,
  Frances, 5
  Elizabeth, 67
  Lucy, 34
  Mary, 51
  Sally, 44, 85

Pierce,
  Clary, 36
  Polly, 15
  Sally B., 80

Pilkington,
  Polly, 50

Pleasant,
  Sally, 40

Pond,
  Hanna, 48

Porter,
  Elizabeth, 26
  Naome, 73
  Scillar, 84
  Sally, 87

Portis,
  Tabitha, 56

Presson,
  Elizabeth, 82
  Hannah, 53
  Lucy, 88
  Mary, 83
  Polly, 23, 82

Preston,
  Lucy, 88

Pretlow,
  Charlotte, 41
  Mary, 42

Price,
  Charity, 31
  Cherry, 31
  Clary, 36
  Dolly, 53
  Hannah, 4
  Lucy, 31
  Martha Ann, 6, 78
  Martha Balmer, 91
  Mildred, 7
  Nancy, 25
  Rebecca R., 78

Pride,
  Mary, 50

Pulley,
  Peggy, 22

Putney,
  Ann Hancock, 3
  Elizabeth, 27, 68
  Mary, 4
  Rebecca, 55

Pyland,
  Betsy, 28
  Elizabeth, 48, 74
  Elizabeth R.P., 52
  Mary B., 48
  Polly P., 62
  Rebecca, 84
  Silviah, 5
  Susan, 22

                R

Rae,
  Nancy, 22
  Susan, 18

Respess,
  Rebecca, 78

Richards,
  Elizabeth, 43
  Hannah, 20
  Rebecca, 21

Riggan,
  Lucy, 46
  Rebecca, 64
  · Rebekah, 66
  Sally, 71
  Susanna, 49

Rispess,
  Mary M., 42
  Nancy, 66
  Rebecca, 78

Roberts,
  Martha, 39

Rogers,
  Ann, 54
  Hannah, 73
  Macy, 43
  Maria, 75
  Martha, 69
  Nancy, 43
  Peggy, 41
  Sarah, 23

Roney,
  Nancy, 27

Rose,
  Elizabeth, 40

Rowell,
  Mary, 52
  Nancy, 52
  Polly (2) 74
  Sally, 45

Ruffin,
  Ann, 52
  Elizabeth, 13, 14
  Hannah, 74
  Martha, 30
  Susanna, 13

                S

St. George,
  Alicia Ann, 75
  Elicea Ann, 75

Salter,
  Betsy, 51
  Mary, 8

Savedge,
  Ann H., 40
  Eliza, 86
  Martha, 5, 42

Savedge, Cont'd.
  Nancy, 75
  Rebecca, 53

Savidge,
  Sucky, 70

Scammell,
  Margaret, 16
  Mary, 38, 45
  Sally, 2

Scott,
  Fanny, 15
  Hannah, 84
  Lucy, 80
  Milley, 81
  Nancy, 26
  Polly, 49, 51
  Tabitha, 15

Seaver,
  Lucinda, 17
  Martha, 46

Sebrell,
  Mary, 80

Seeds,
  Ann, 30

Seward,
  Elizabeth, 35
  Elizabeth N., 78
  Martha, 69
  Mary, 47
  Polly M., 15
  Sally H., 8
  Rebecca, 69, 70

Shackleford,
  Elizabeth, 79

Shackleton,
  Elizabeth, 79

Sharp,
  Elizabeth S., 87
  Mary, 58
  Sarah, 32
  Susan, 44

Shearman,
  Mary, 5

Sheffield,
  Anne, 50
  Elizabeth, 25
  Matilda, 60
  Nancy, 50, 80
  Rebecca, 11
  Susanna, 59

Shell,
  Lucy, 14

Shelly,
  Cynthia, 62
  Eliza, 47

Short,
  Martha, 29

Shuffield,
  Elizabeth, 69
  Winney, 6

Simmons,
  Mary, 58
  Polly, 58
  Sally, 52, 86

Sinclair,
  Margaret M., 12

Slade,
  Ann, 4
  Betsy, 77
  Elizabeth, 77
  Keziah, 10
  Lucy, 72
  Malicy, 62
  Nancy, 92
  Peggy, 48
  Rebecca, 13
  Sally, 13, 14
  Susanna, 35

Slate,
  Susan, 65

Sledge,
  Ann, 27
  Dolly, 10
  Elizabeth, 80

Smalley,
  Elizabeth, 47

Smedle,
  Sarah, 17

Smith,
  Averilla, 88
  Betsy, 62
  Charity, 35
  Elizabeth C., 20
  Elizabeth E., 21
  Maranda, 92
  Marenda, 92
  Martha, 1
  Mary, 62
  Mary Ann, 42
  Nancy, 70
  Rebecca, 15
  Sally E., 37
  Sally T., 66
  Sarah, 36
  Susan, 19, 21
  Susanna, 73

Solloman,
  Sally, 36

Solomon,
  Lucy, 49

Sorsby,
  Ann, 25
  Elizabeth, 25
  Mary, 57
  Rebecca, 8
  Sarah, 41, 59
  Susanna, 11, 78

Southall,
  Susan, 28

Spratley,
  Ann, 33, 53
  Rebecca Young, 26

Stacy,
  Nancy, 15

Stephens,
  Ariana, 18
  Martha, 70
  Sarah, 17

Stevens,
  Elizabeth, 65